MONICA SULLIVAN

James Sullivan is the author of *Jeans* and a regular contributor to *The Boston Globe*. He previously served as the pop music and culture critic at the *San Francisco Chronicle* and has written for many other publications. He lives in Massachusetts.

THE HARDEST WORKING MAN

★ ★ ★ ★ ★ ★ ★ ★

HOW
JAMES BROWN
SAVED THE
—SOUL—
OF AMERICA

JAMES SULLIVAN

GOTHAM BOOKS

GOTHAM BOOKS
Published by Penguin Group (USA) Inc.
375 Hudson Street, New York, New York 10014, U.S.A.

Penguin Group (Canada), 90 Eglinton Avenue East, Suite 700, Toronto, Ontario M4P 2Y3, Canada (a division of Pearson Penguin Canada Inc.); Penguin Books Ltd, 80 Strand, London WC2R 0RL, England; Penguin Ireland, 25 St Stephen's Green, Dublin 2, Ireland (a division of Penguin Books Ltd); Penguin Group (Australia), 250 Camberwell Road, Camberwell, Victoria 3124, Australia (a division of Pearson Australia Group Pty Ltd); Penguin Books India Pvt Ltd, 11 Community Centre, Panchsheel Park, New Delhi–110 017, India; Penguin Group (NZ), 67 Apollo Drive, Rosedale, North Shore 0632, New Zealand (a division of Pearson New Zealand Ltd); Penguin Books (South Africa) (Pty) Ltd, 24 Sturdee Avenue, Rosebank, Johannesburg 2196, South Africa

Penguin Books Ltd, Registered Offices: 80 Strand, London WC2R 0RL, England

Published by Gotham Books, a member of Penguin Group (USA) Inc.

Previously published as a Gotham Books hardcover edition.

First trade paperback printing, November 2009

10 9 8 7 6 5 4 3

Gotham Books and the skyscraper logo are trademarks of Penguin Group (USA) Inc.

The Library of Congress has cataloged the hardcover edition of this book as follows:

Sullivan, James, 1965 Nov. 7–
    The hardest working man: how James Brown saved the soul of America: live at the Boston Garden, 1968 / James Sullivan.
        p. cm.
    ISBN: 978-1-592-40390-5 (hardcover)   ISBN: 978-1-592-40490-2 (paperback)   1. Brown, James, 1933–2006.   2. Soul musicians—United States—Biography.   I. Title.
    ML420.B818S85 2008
    782.421644092—dc22
    [B]   2008013670

Printed in the United States of America
Set in Goudy Oldstyle
Designed by Jessica Shatan Heslin/Studio Shatan, Inc.

While the author has made every effort to provide accurate telephone numbers and Internet addresses at the time of publication, neither the publisher nor the author assumes any responsibility for errors, or for changes that occur after publication. Further, the publisher does not have any control over and does not assume any responsibility for author or third-party Web sites or their content.

To my father—
our very own Papa

CONTENTS

FOREWORD

I remember the initial impact the Godfather had on me. In my mind I can still see myself and my second-grade peers slipping and sliding on the frozen patches of winter ice in Queens, New York. The thing that kept our balance was the rhythm of doing the "James Brown," the dance that Mr. JB had claimed for his own bad self at the end of "There Was a Time." The energy of Mr. JB's music was the bottled power of elementary school kids running wild. Just line 'em up at the schoolyard door . . . and open it. They have no idea where they're headed—they just go. That, for me, describes the fuel of James Brown. Yes, James Brown was a man, but he had the boundless spark of a kid.

My parents kept a lot of records in the crib. They were a hip twentysomething black couple surrounded by times of turbulence. The records came bundled from the mail-order record clubs, so there were a lot of jazz discs, comedy, and soul. James Brown's records had a lot of colors, courtesy of the King Records art department. Them records jumped out at you, but not nearly as much as

JB's scream, and that rhythm section, on the albums inside. JAMES BROWN stood out from the pack—outta sight *and* sound.

My grandmother used to subscribe to *Look* magazine, and *Life*. She and my grandfather tended to stack magazines, not records. It was *Look* that asked the question about Mr. JB—was he "the most important black man in America"? The cover was bluish, I remember. This was smack-dab in the middle of Vietnam, on the edges of the murders of Dr. Martin Luther King, Jr., and Robert F. Kennedy. It was an eerie echo of just a few years back, when President John F. Kennedy and Malcolm X were murdered. The country needed a common language about this madness going down—why shouldn't it come from the cultural icons everyone listened to? But on the heels of the riots in Newark and Detroit, I guess dancing in the streets couldn't be delivered to the people by Motown, Stax, Atlantic, or anyone else but JB. After the release of "Say It Loud—I'm Black and I'm Proud," the government—especially a J. Edgar Hoover government—happened to understand the importance of JB for many reasons, both good and bad. The fact that mayors, politicians, the military, presidents, and vice presidents reached out to JB, while pop stations and the musical mainstream cut him off, is a piece of mind-boggling irony. That one song earned Mr. JB a lucky seven more years of black love from the 'hood, and that don't come easy.

In my humble opinion, Mr. James Brown was the most powerful black man in the immediate aftermath of the assassination of MLK. Blackfolk were looking for many answers on this ball of confusion in 1968. All Americans were looking for answers with baffled faces, but the black impulse was on a national Nat Turner vibe. I heard about the Boston Garden concert way after the fact. Being seven years old in New York at the time, the news for me was dealing with New York's issues and its own potential to blow up. I didn't go to school much that week. Boston was an afterthought, especially at a time when the emphasis was on local news and there was only a peephole each night for national and world news. Sportswise, the Celtics were coming back to get Wilt's 76ers, but first black coach Bill Russell's take on the racism problem in Boston added fuel to the speculation that there might be some local noise, tired of newenglandwhitey.

We live in a much different time today, and I'm not talking racially. I'm speaking technologically. Cable, documentaries, DVDs, bootlegs, YouTube, and the Internet have allowed thousands to check the actual vibe of the concert broadcast that night at the Boston Garden. I'm still tripping today on the fact that this was a live broadcast designed to keep people off them Beantown streets. Paranoia until there's an answer, is what I call it. The James Brown Show was and is, to me, the incredible effect of music and willpower to freeze all else, for the joy of being entertained as one, by one, on the One. The footage carries the tension of a 1960s Hurricane Katrina. Hypnotizing. Paralyzing. Tantalizing. And yet he stopped and got everyone to "Think," as yet another of JB's many hits preached.

No doubt the Godfather of Soul doubled as the ultimate Prince of Peace in a time of chaos. In fact, we're still doubled over by this amazing showing, which grows in such significance by the decade.

Chuck D
PUBLIC ENEMY
January 2008

If Elvis Presley / is King,
Who is James Brown,
God?

Amiri Baraka, *"In the Funk World"*

THE HARDEST
WORKING MAN

OVERTURE

His mere presence was tumultuous, like freak weather. His singing, of course, was volcanic; his dancing, like a cyclone. There scarcely seems any other way to describe it: James Brown was a force of nature. "He came on like the aurora borealis," with red, white, and blue spotlights splashing across the purple tuxedos of his eighteen-piece band, wrote a stunned correspondent for *Time* magazine in 1966, a decade after "Please Please Please," the singer's first hit. For a delirious crowd of fifteen thousand at Madison Square Garden, Brown "commanded the stage like a one-man riot."

Eliciting such superlatives was James Brown's stock in trade. He was, undoubtedly, an innovator of rhythm and a mighty performer, but he was also a peerless self-promoter. "I'm looking for something that nobody else does," he said. He marched through life under a flashing marquee of outrageously self-serving nicknames: The Godfather of Soul! Soul Brother Number One! Mr. Dynamite! Butane James! He compared himself to "those cats" Mozart, Bach, Beethoven, Strauss. He costumed himself as a black Superman, or a gaudy emperor. He considered himself a distinctly American hero.

A child of brutal poverty and neglect who reveled in his own Horatio Alger story—the shoeshine boy outside the radio station who later bought the station—Brown was pride personified. He was the original ghetto superstar, exulting in his identity as Langston Hughes's "darker brother." "They'll see how beautiful I am / And be ashamed," as the poet had predicted, and Brown lived out Hughes's promise: "I, too, sing America." By the late 1960s, senators and presidents—men who made their livings with their mouths—had come to recognize that Brown's supernatural voice was an instrument without parallel. "Is he the most important black man in America?" asked *Look* magazine.

Though Brown's career was born at nearly the same moment as rock 'n' roll, though he all but invented soul and funk, the bands he led might compare most closely with the jazz orchestra of Duke Ellington. In both cases, the music was scrupulously arranged yet designed to stimulate transcendent improvisation. Ellington's *Black, Brown and Beige* was the abbreviated version of his grand plans for a jazz opera called *Boola*, the ageless title character of which he imagined as a mythic representation of the entire African-American experience. What Ellington started, James Brown finished. Brown, it might be argued, *was* Boola—from Emancipation to self-determination, from vaudeville to bop to hip-hop.

In the pop music era, only Elvis Presley placed more songs in *Billboard*'s Hot 100, and no act but the Beatles has come close to matching the multigenerational longevity of Brown's influence. Yet his true gift was not so much any particular God-given talent or stylistic permutation. It was the steel strength of his will. The thing about James Brown was this: He refused to take no for an answer.

A "one-man riot" of positive thinking, James Brown had no use for the blues. Descended from slavery-era spirituals and work songs, the blues were "sorrow songs," in the words of Frederick Douglass and W. E. B. Du Bois. "This is going to surprise a lot of people: I still don't like the blues. Never have," Brown declared in his autobiography, published in 1986. His was a self-confidence so supreme that it bordered on the absurd. Sorrow was not permitted in James Brown's music. Indignation, maybe; an occasional apoplectic fit. Never abject sorrow. That sheer indomitability is James Brown's crucial contribution to American culture.

Ralph Waldo Emerson described heroism as a "military attitude of the soul." The hero, he noted, is not without faults. He can be bullheaded, self-absorbed, not given to reflection. "There is somewhat [sic] not philosophical in heroism," Emerson wrote. "There is somewhat not holy in it; it seems not to know that other souls are of one texture with it; it hath pride; it is the extreme of individual nature. . . . Heroism feels and never reasons, and therefore is always right."

Like many other gifted individuals, James Brown's ego and his appetites were as heroic as his attitude. His private life was, by any measure, no match for his upright public image. Lacking any capacity to accept the inevitable diminishment of his pop stardom, his later years were particularly troubled. Arrests, affairs, illegitimate children, substance abuse, domestic violence, tax evasion: the list of his transgressions would have staggered Stagger Lee.

For James Brown—the Hardest Working Man in Show Business—the life he lived offstage was the one that felt unreal. All of his extraordinary energy went into the construction and maintenance of his image. Out of the public eye, he was no role model. Onstage, however, he was a modern-day folk hero.

"James Brown is a concept, a vibration, a dance," as he put it. "It's not me, the man. James Brown is a freedom I created for humanity." During his heyday—the decade beginning in mid-1964, when he began to alter the course of pop music with his emphatic, almost belligerent newness—he epitomized freedom and opportunity in America. It was no coincidence that the time of his greatest relevance was also the era of the civil rights struggle. It was, as Brown's music would attest, a new day.

In the hours after the assassination of Dr. King, it was a rare American who could have felt that way.

★ ★ ★ I ★ ★ ★

LOST SOMEONE

The back of his jacket is soaked through with sweat. His beloved hair, carefully plastered to his skull before he took the stage, now shoots maniacally toward the rafters. For two hours, as always, the dynamo at center stage has imposed his colossal will on his audience— shrieking and thrashing, as a sideman once noted, as if he were literally plugged into his spectacular band.

"Please! Please. Please," roars James Brown. For the thousandth time, the horns blare dementedly; the guitarist jangles the chord changes; the drummer punishes his snare. The backup singers bellow the supporting vocal as if it were a drunken pirate shanty. And the crowd comes unhinged.

Every one of Brown's concerts ends in bedlam like this, as fans of the unstoppable soul singer succumb to the fever pitch of his convulsive signature song. For once, however, his customary showstopping plea is no mere act.

Outside, the worst American rioting of the twentieth century is well under way. Almost every major metropolitan area across the country has erupted in vandalism, arson, looting. The city of Boston, where Brown is performing, is in virtual lockdown. It is the fifth of April, 1968, twenty-four hours after the murder of Dr. Martin Luther King, Jr., and one hardheaded entertainer at the pinnacle of his persuasive power is attempting to shout down the madness.

As his big band brawls its way through the song, the frontman bends back at the waist and lets out a truly astonishing scream. It is the sound of a man—or a woman—who has just encountered the ghastliest sight of a lifetime.

The exertion twists Brown's torso to the right, and he collapses to his knees. Roadie Kenny Hull, who looks not unlike Muhammad Ali in his formal wear and his well-tended natural hairstyle, is the night's designated attendant. He hustles to Brown's side and drapes the singer in a luxurious spangled cape, helps him to his feet, pats his back. The singer, according to the time-tested artifice of the James Brown Revue, violently throws off the cape. Revived, he rushes back to the microphone and screams. Words are utterly beside the point, too precious. The thing is to be heard. Brown, more than anyone, refuses not to be.

He's down again, buckling under a great weight. The second cape is striped. When this one is thrown off, so too goes the dinner jacket. Brown stomps back to the microphone, his suspenders and the piping on his pants shimmering in the light. Repeatedly, violently, he lifts a knee and pulls the mic stand toward him, as if simultaneously yanking a man's coat over his shoulders and delivering a blow to his gut. More than ever, "Please Please Please" is not about a lover; it's about loss, and survival, about a desperate craving for adulation, about tenacity in the face of adversity.

*One more time with another bejeweled robe. This time, it's white.
As Brown strolls back toward center stage, a young man leaps up
from the floor and is quickly shoved back by a bodyguard. The stage
is immediately filled with handlers and policemen, all of them brac-
ing for a real disturbance. This is not the first overzealous fan of the
evening to clamber onstage. Brown, blowing kisses, works himself
up front, looks with disdain over his shoulder at the officers, waves
both arms in their direction like flippers, as if to say, "Step aside. I'll
handle this."*

*With a contemplative lean forward and a pantomime crack on a
snare, the singer cues the rising guitar notes and bubbling organ that
signal his recent release, "I Can't Stand Myself (When You Touch
Me)." Another young man in a windbreaker hauls himself over the
lip of the stage and lunges for Brown. Before his hand reaches the
singer, an officer presses him back into the crowd. The tension is fast
becoming unbearable.*

*"Can't stand it. Can't stand your love," Brown sings, then de-
cides he's seen enough. "Wait a minute," he grumbles, and the band
quickly peters off into silence.*

*"Move over," the singer tells the police. "I'll be all right. I'll be
fine." A boy, not five feet tall, in a flat cap and an overcoat, suddenly materializes behind him.*

*"You are my man, baby," he tells Brown in a soft but clear
voice.*

*"You want to dance, son?" Brown asks, and the boy grins.
"Dance."*

*Instantly there are a half-dozen, then a dozen fans surrounding
the singer. The boy makes a high-stepping move, pulling his wrists together at chest level, then popping his collar. There is no music, only
the loud murmur of confusion. A young man turns to the audience*

and waves for everyone to join him onstage. "Wait a minute. Wait a minute, here!" Brown complains. The Hardest Working Man in Show Business is not at all accustomed to watching his own show get away from him. "Let me finish the show for everybody else. . . . Y'all go down, now. Go down, fellas. Go down now."

This is not the way the concert was supposed to go. Earlier, Brown had shared the stage with the mayor of Boston, who'd worked frantically with the singer and city officials throughout the day to arrange for the show to be broadcast on local television. It was at once a calculated distraction and a conciliatory gesture toward the city's black population. At the microphone, Kevin White had risen to the occasion. Let us look at each other, he had told the crowds at the Boston Garden and in surrounding homes, "and pledge that no matter what any other community might do, we in Boston will honor Dr. King in peace."

Now, however, the threat of violence was palpable. The police are on edge; the young men in the front rows seem to be taunting their authority. Around greater Boston, viewers are appalled at the prospect of yet another ugly incident in this grim decade playing itself out on live television.

But Brown simply isn't willing to stand by as the event explodes into conflict. "Wait. Wait a minute!" he repeats again and again. "This—is no way. We are black. We are black! . . . Don't make us all look bad!" In a flash, his attention has shifted from the aggression of the police to the behavior of his own fans.

The seconds are as endless as those of an earthquake tremor. Though he is clearly agitated, for James Brown, the consummate performer, no situation is too bleak. The show . . . must . . . go . . . on.

"Step down now," Brown says to the young boy, who finally

*obliges. "Be a gentleman." For the moment, at least, he has regained
control.*

*"Now are we together, or are we ain't?" asks the singer, unable
to hide his exasperation. He's talking to his fans. He's talking to the
police. Most of all, he is talking to his country.*

*For once, James Brown is genuinely drained. There is no chore-
ography in it.*

*"Hit the thing, man," he mutters to his drummer. "Huh. Can't
stand it."*

Early April 1968: Star time for James Brown. After more
than ten years of dominance on the rhythm and blues
charts, selling records by the boxful and packing theaters
and auditoriums across black America, the self-styled Mr. Dynamite was in the process of dismantling pop music and re-creating
it in his own image. He had finally seized a sizable portion of the
mainstream for himself with five top ten hits in less than three
years, sandwiching a "new breed" of rhythmically explosive songs
that would inspire entire genres—"Papa's Got a Brand New
Bag," "I Got You (I Feel Good)," "Cold Sweat," "I Got the Feelin' "—around an extravagant ballad, "It's a Man's Man's Man's
World." Already the stuff of legend was his otherworldly turn on
The T.A.M.I. Show, a kinescopic 1964 concert film featuring the
Beach Boys, the Rolling Stones, the Supremes, and other teen
idols. (The show's name was an acronym for Teenage Awards
Music International, or, alternately, Teen Age Music International.) Rock 'n' roll lore has it that Brown's dazzling singing and
dancing during filming at the Santa Monica Civic Auditorium
left a young Mick Jagger, who was scheduled to follow him on
the bill, slackjawed.

After *The T.A.M.I. Show*, word of Brown's unrivaled stage presence spread quickly, earning him repeat appearances on programs such as *American Bandstand* (where he had made his national television debut at the beginning of the decade), *Where the Action Is,* and *The Ed Sullivan Show.* Now, widely recognized as an incandescent soul man with a pronounced show-biz flair that Sinatra fans could appreciate, he was working on a syndicated television special to be called *James Brown: Man to Man.*

The hour-long program would feature footage of the performer and his band onstage at Harlem's Apollo Theater, the site of his most sensational, career-defining performances. His first *Live at the Apollo* album, released in 1963, was the sound of a man with an unfathomable ability to hold both his audience and his musicians in utter thrall. Like Ellington before him, Brown's organization of his ever-changing backing band was the product of a masterly musical mind. The attention of a great conductor "is everywhere at once," wrote Elias Canetti in *Crowds and Power,* translated into English in 1962. "He is inside the mind of every player. He knows not only what each *should* be doing, but also what he *is* doing. He is the living embodiment of law, both positive and negative. . . . Since, during the performance, nothing is supposed to exist except this work, for so long is the conductor the ruler of the world."

Brown certainly sounds like the ruler of the world on the original *Live at the Apollo,* careening from half-whispered exhortations to wildcat howls as the audience shrieks as though they're on the Coney Island Cyclone. Ruling, for Brown, came naturally. Musicians were his troops, to be whipped into shape. Audiences were there for the conquering. Competitors—other soul stars of the 1960s, from Sam Cooke to Joe Tex and Solomon Burke—were enemy forces to be vanquished. When a high school kid from Cleveland began making flashy clothes for the red-hot Al Green, Brown stole him away. It was no accident that one of Brown's favorite songs to perform was "If I Ruled the World," a soapy ballad plucked from the Broadway musical *Pickwick* by way of Tony Bennett's hit recording. For Brown, the song appealed, somewhat paradoxically, to both his insatiable lust for power and his genuine social concern: "If I ruled the world, every man would be as free as a bird / Every voice would be a voice to be heard."

That's how he opened the Apollo concert for *Man to Man*, in full Copacabana mode, perched on a stool in a white turtleneck and baby blue dinner jacket, his hair a little less elaborately sculpted than usual, a dark soul patch clinging to his bottom lip. The interstitial footage featured the ever-impeccable singer in a Nehru jacket, walking alone through condemned inner-city neighborhoods, looking grave. "I want you to know that I'm more than just an artist, a man that sing[s] and dance[s] and scream[s] or something on the stage," he says, uncharacteristically subdued, in a voice-over. "I want you to know that I'm a man—a black man. A soul brother." This simple declaration, made for national television in early 1968, amounted to radical politics for a man intent on claiming the mantle of show-business superstardom. True, rock bands had begun to express their dissatisfaction with the status quo and their opposition to the war in Vietnam, and some soul singers were addressing the civil rights movement in generalized terms, writing about imminent change and the dream of living in harmony. But Brown, just a few years removed from performing for segregated crowds, was poised to make his very blackness a commodity.

Until then, blackness had been a condition to overcome, not amplify. It had been two years since Stokely Carmichael's call for "black power," which brought the term out of the shadows—but also set white America on its heels. In fact, African-Americans had been called "black," at least colloquially, for decades; W. E. B. Du Bois's classic collection of essays, *The Souls of Black Folk*, was first published in 1903. Richard Wright's *Black Boy* was published in 1945, and American culture by the mid-1960s was becoming saturated with the term. Langston Hughes's *Black Nativity* opened on Broadway in 1961, coinciding with the publication of *Black Like Me*, journalist John Howard Griffin's provocative study of racial inequality in the South. But blackness was just beginning to achieve popular acceptance. For lifetimes, it had been considered a pejorative. "To call somebody black was an insult," as Cab Calloway once recalled, "and of course, to call me black, light-skinned as I was, was a triple insult." "My community was afraid of that word," said the boxer George Foreman, who grew up in Texas. Brown agreed: "When I was growin' up, if somebody called me 'black' that had an ignorance thing to it."

By the late 1960s, however, James Brown—a powerful black man in the time of Black Power—identified proudly with the term. But the civil rights movement, having come such a long way, still had a long way to go. "I guess I'm real concerned about people," Brown said in *Man to Man*, narrating the footage of himself surveying the ghettos. "Torn buildings. The buildings that are still standing but should be removed. Know who lives there? The black people . . . My fight is against the past—the old colored man. My fight now is for the black American to become American."

While Brown was working on his television special—for all intents and purposes, his national introduction as a socially conscious entertainer—the Rev. Martin Luther King, Jr., was in Memphis, the home of the blues. The two men had known each other for years, often crossing paths in their home state of Georgia. Though Brown admired the civil rights champion, he thought of himself as a truer representative of the working-class black man. "Dr. King himself wasn't a street person," as he would recall. "I was. I came from a ghetto and was close to the people in the ghettos all over America."

On a rainy evening in Memphis, King addressed a crowd of thousands in support of striking city sanitation workers at the Mason Temple Church. The beleaguered rights leader had not been himself in the weeks prior to Memphis. His brand of nonviolent protest was being ridiculed as ineffective and emasculating by a younger generation of culture warriors. Lately the minister had been struggling to align his own views with those of the more radical left—and developing an acute sense of his own impending demise. In an eloquent speech in which he referred to his fellow African-Americans as "colored" and "Negro"—but also, at more than one point, "black"—Dr. King entwined calls for black unity and boycotts of unfavorable businesses (such as Coca-Cola and Wonder Bread) with an uncanny reflection on his own mortality. Famous for its climactic "I've been to the mountaintop" flourish, the speech recalled the incident of the minister's stabbing a few years prior. Of all the correspondence he received while recuperating in the hospital, he told his vociferous audience, the one he cherished most came from a ninth-grade schoolgirl who had read that the wound was so close to his aorta, one sneeze would have killed him. "I'm simply writing to say to you that I'm so happy that you didn't sneeze," she'd written.

His own mortality, King suggested, was no longer such a concern to him. But his life's work, the civil rights movement, was at a critical juncture. "Nothing," he cried, "would be more tragic than to stop at this point, in Memphis."

Less than twenty-four hours later, just after six o'clock in the evening on Thursday, the fourth of April, Dr. King was assassinated, dropped by a sniper's single bullet to the neck as he stepped onto the balcony of his second-floor room in the Lorraine Motel. In a hideous instant, the movement itself seemed to have been gunned down.

★ ★ ★ 2 ★ ★ ★

BEWILDERED

THE MINISTER OF PEACE IS SLAIN, blurted the morning headline in *The Boston Globe*, in the city of King's education. As everywhere across the nation, there was "despair in the streets." Groups of enraged young men were reported roaming the city's predominantly African-American neighborhoods of Roxbury, Dorchester, and the South End. Overnight, there were an estimated thirteen injuries and dozens of people taken into custody by the Boston police, which was augmented in the Grove Hall area of Roxbury by fifty members of the Tactical Patrol Force. Parked cars were overturned and set afire; storefronts were smashed and looted. Despite the arrival of a drizzling rain at around two o'clock in the morning, agitated throngs and vigilant police officers remained on the streets as the newspaper went to press in the wee hours.

Boston, as the *Globe* noted in an accompanying story, was

King's "second home." In 1955, four years after completing his Bachelor of Divinity degree at Crozer Theological Seminary in Pennsylvania, he earned his Doctor of Philosophy from Boston University, where he studied systematic theology. During his years in Boston, King met and courted his future wife, Coretta Scott, a student at the New England Conservatory of Music. "I feel very strongly that I was *sent* to Boston, directed there," Mrs. King would write, "because it was in Boston that I met Martin Luther King, Jr."

Years after departing Boston with his new bride for his ministry in Montgomery, Alabama, Dr. King brought his message of nonviolent resistance back to Boston, in April of 1965. Thousands marched with the minister, by this time an internationally renowned figure, three miles from the Carter Playground in Roxbury to the Boston Common. "One of the greatest days that Boston has ever seen," he called it.

Boston, sometimes called the "abolitionist city" and the "cradle of liberty," had a noble history of support for the rights of African-Americans. Though Massachusetts had been the first colony to legalize slavery, in 1641, it was also the first to abolish it, in 1783. The first anti-slavery argument in the colonies was published in 1700 by Samuel Sewall, a Harvard-educated Puritan and Massachusetts judge. Bostonian Phillis Wheatley became the first African-American writer to publish, in 1773. In the late 1820s David Walker, a free black man born in North Carolina, used his clothing shop on Boston's Brattle Street as a clearinghouse for his controversial seventy-six-page pamphlet, *Walker's Appeal . . . to the Coloured Citizens of the World*, which called for a slave rebellion. When Walker arranged to have copies smuggled into the South, several states put a bounty on the tailor's head and made possession of his treatise punishable by death. Boston was a city, as one writer has noted, "that slaves heard about, dreamed about, and around which they planned their escapes."

As the new nation bitterly debated the institution of slavery, social reformer William Lloyd Garrison took center stage in the abolition movement with his newspaper *The Liberator*, published in Boston for thirty-five years beginning in 1831. "Assenting to the 'self-evident truth' maintained in the American Declaration of Independence, 'that all men are created equal, and endowed by their Creator with certain inalienable rights—among which are life, liberty, and the pursuit of happiness,' " Garrison wrote in an open letter in the *Liberator*'s inaugural issue, "I shall strenuously contend for the immediate enfranchisement of our slave population." Other prominent Bostonians joined the cause, among them Emerson. When Massachusetts senator Charles Sumner, another influential abolitionist, was brutally attacked with a gold-tipped cane by South Carolina senator Preston Brooks on the Senate floor in Washington, D.C., Emerson was incensed. "We must get rid of slavery," he said, "or we must get rid of freedom."

As late as the 1940s, the city of Boston was, relatively speaking, fairly progressive with regard to its black population. Malcolm X, in his *Autobiography*, noted with some amusement that black Boston had its own "snooty" enclave to compare with those of the blue-blood Brahmins. The residents of Roxbury's Waumbeck and Humboldt Avenue Hill section, where the teenager, then known as Malcolm Little, arrived in 1940 to live with his half-sister Ella, "called themselves the 'Four Hundred,' and looked down their noses at the Negroes of the black ghetto."

Another newcomer, Edward Brooke, claimed to have encountered no discrimination in Boston's restaurants and theaters during his years of study at Boston University Law School, from which he graduated in 1948. "I could go where I pleased," recalled Brooke, a native of Washington, D.C., who went on to become the first black United States senator elected by popular vote, as a Massachusetts Republican in 1966.

But despite all this Boston, like almost every other northern city, had lapsed into increasingly uneasy race relations by the 1960s. Waves of black families were rapidly transforming neighborhoods formerly occupied by white ethnic groups, who were dispatching to the suburbs by the thousands. In a compact geographical city of less than seven hundred thousand residents—down dramatically from a peak of eight hundred thousand in 1950—ninety thousand blacks had settled by 1967. That figure represented twice the number of black Bostonians just five years earlier.

The population shift coincided with the continuation of an aggressive urban renewal program overseen by the Boston Redevelopment Authority (BRA), which had begun in the 1940s with the demolition of Scollay Square and the Old West End. Outraged residents of endangered neighborhoods in the South End and Roxbury bitterly nicknamed the BRA the "Black Removal Authority." Meanwhile, the sensitive question of school desegregation would emerge as the defining issue of the 1967 mayoral campaign between matronly Boston School Committee member Louise Day Hicks and Massachusetts Secretary of State Kevin White, a graduate of Boston College Law School and the Harvard Graduate School of Public Administration (now the John F. Kennedy School of Government). Hicks, the eventual loser, would nevertheless gain national notoriety in the coming decade for her rallying role in white Boston's vehement opposition to busing programs designed to facilitate integration. Her thinly veiled campaign slogan reflected the city's increasingly caustic polarization: "You know where I stand."

After sidestepping the urban disturbances that roiled Detroit, the Watts section of Los Angeles, and other urban areas in the summers of 1964–66, Boston experienced its own civil unrest in 1967. The flashpoint proved to be the sensitive subject of welfare. In late spring a group calling itself Mothers for Adequate Welfare locked themselves inside a Roxbury district office of the welfare department, protesting what they felt were inadequate funds and open hostility on the part of the staff. When police attempted to remove the estimated thirty protesters, one of them screamed, and the crowd gathered outside began to riot. Cars were overturned, storefronts smashed, fires set. One fireman was shot in the hand. After three nights of skirmishing, sixty-three arrests had been made, with thirty officers and many more citizens reporting injuries. Boston, as *Time* magazine put it, had "finally succumbed to ghetto dementia."

"If the police don't get out of Roxbury," one mother, holding an infant, told a *Globe* reporter, "this rioting is going to go on forever." Other residents, however, attributed the violence and vandalism to the restlessness of youth more than any social protest: "It's the kids' bag," said one man.

That autumn, Boston's mayoral race would be decided over the precarious prospects for racial conciliation. White, an Irish-Catholic native Bostonian with quite a pedigree in local politics—his father, his father-in-law, and his maternal grandfather had all served as Boston City Council presidents—ran on a platform of economic rehabilitation, promising social services and advocating rent control. The urban renewal advances of the previous administration, he said, now required "people programs to match the building programs." In the newspaper's first political endorsement in decades, a jittery *Globe* identified White as the candidate best suited to assuage animosities in the lower-income neighborhoods. After taking office in January, the new mayor declared City Hall open twenty-four hours a day, announced a plan to modernize the police department, and broke ground on a unique outreach effort based around neighborhood service centers called Little City Halls. Seemingly every move he made was designed to ease concerns over "white flight" and black insurrection. "My job is to keep this city cool," he said.

But no amount of foresight could have prepared him for the agonizing events that would be set in motion on the evening of April fourth. When news of the King assassination came in, the mayor was sitting in a darkened downtown movie theater, watching old Georgia burn in a revival screening of *Gone with the Wind*.

★ ★ ★ 3 ★ ★ ★

THINK

The Boston Tea Party was just gathering momentum in April 1968. Named for the infamous anti-tax rebellion in Boston Harbor at the dawn of the American Revolution, the Tea Party, a ballroom-style nightclub in a onetime Unitarian meeting house on Berkeley Street in Boston's South End, was fast becoming the college town's premier stage for rock 'n' roll "dance concerts," as they were called at the time.

The year-old Tea Party was the live music venture of a bohemian coffeehouse, initially called the Moondial, which was intended for avant-garde film screenings. The Filmmakers Cinematheque was founded by Mel Lyman, harmonica player of the folk-revival Kweskin Jug Band and leader of a commune-style "family" based in the Fort Hill neighborhood of Roxbury. The project showcased the experimental work of filmmakers such as Andy Warhol, Stan Brakhage, and Kenneth Anger. The live shows, featuring such local acts as the Lost and the Hallucinations, were developed to augment the modest box office receipts of the film program. As the film series withered, the Tea Party took over, becoming a favored tour stop for progressive rock acts such as the Velvet Underground and Van Morrison. Modeled after the Fillmore Auditorium and the Avalon Ballroom in San Francisco, the cathedral-style hippie hangout featured plenty of blues and R&B acts alongside the psychedelic guitar bands.

Initially, the club was open only on Fridays and Saturdays. The fourth of April, a Thursday, marked the debut of an expanded schedule that would include weekdays. To celebrate, club manager Steve Nelson had booked Chicago electric blues giant Muddy Waters, a hero to the new generation of roaring, hard-blues-worshipping would-be rock stars. Muddy was a presence, and he had his full band with him, featuring pianist Otis Spann and harmonica player Little Walter. But as darkness settled, the quiet, anticipatory bustle of preparing a concert hall for business was shattered when word arrived that Martin Luther King had been shot and killed just after six o'clock in the Memphis evening, after stepping out onto the balcony of his second-floor room at the Lorraine Motel.

Disbelieving neighbors across the country instantly began spilling into the streets, spreading the terrible news. Dana Chandler, a politically charged painter and artist who was then a familiar figure in Boston as an activist, was at home with his family on Moreland Street. When he saw the news of the assassination on television, he stormed out of the house, venting his fury by smashing a nearby phone booth with his fists. Outbursts such as Chandler's brought almost instantaneous response from the Boston police department, which was on high alert after the disturbances of the previous summer. A patroling officer aimed his .38 at the artist and shouted at him to settle down.

Driving down Roxbury's Blue Hill Avenue about an hour after the murder, a young white man was dragged from his car and severely beaten. As the crowd labored to overturn his car, which they eventually set on fire, two neighborhood activists pulled up in a YMCA panel truck. Bill Wimberly, director of the new Roxbury YMCA on Warren Street, and Marvin Butler, the Y's community program director, hauled the injured man into the back of the van and sped off. The victim, horrified, jumped out of the back of the vehicle and began to run. Wimberly and Butler, fearing for his life, called the police department and asked them to find the man. "It was not safe to be a white man in Roxbury," Wimberly recounted for a reporter a few days later. By then, neither he nor Butler had slept much since the breaking news of King's murder. Like other community leaders, they worked around the clock that weekend, pleading for peace. The journalist noted that Butler's white armband, hastily fashioned from a handkerchief, was soiled.

King's assassination, biographer Marshall Frady would write, seemed "almost a personal enactment of the death of the non-violent movement in America." "There must be a better way of settling our differences than shooting each other," one woman told *The Boston Globe*. "People are disenchanted," said another resident, a man in thick glasses and a small fedora named McDonald Gittens. "They don't believe in gradualism anymore." Across the country, cities were erupting in spontaneous acts of violence and vandalism. Bitterness and rage would not be contained. Rioting, as King himself had said, was the "the language of the unheard." In the immediate aftermath of his murder, it seemed likely to be the dominant language. The political philosophy of moderation, already imperiled with the rise of the movement's more radical offshoots, suddenly seemed even to many of its strictest adherents a hopelessly outdated tactic.

Inside the Boston Tea Party, Steve Nelson was staggered. Before coming to Boston to attend Harvard Law School, he'd gone to Cornell University with a sociology major named Michael Schwerner. Their parents were best friends. In June 1964, Schwerner was murdered in Philadelphia, Mississippi, along with two fellow CORE field workers, James Chaney and Andrew Goodman, while promoting voter registration in the Deep South. For Nelson, each of the subsequent murders of the civil rights era hit hard.

Though Muddy Waters and his band were similarly devastated, everyone involved quickly decided to go ahead with the show, in tribute to Dr. King. The Tea Party already had a reputation for drawing an integrated crowd. Just two weeks later B.B. King would headline the club in his first Boston appearance outside the black theater circuit. Young people from the mixed South End frequented the place, which had no liquor license and a cheap three-dollar cover charge. Everyone who entered the room came for the music, which, on this night, would prove to be heartrending.

The opening act was the Hallucinations, who were fronted by Peter Wolf, a fast-talking hipster who had just become one of the first on-air talents with WBCN, a failing classical station that had begun licensing its overnight hours to Tea Party owner Ray Riepen. Wolf, who would go on to stardom with the J. Geils Band, was a great fan of the blues. He had befriended Waters and his musicians on their previous visits to the city, lending his apartment off Harvard Square as a makeshift dressing room. To Nelson, the Waters band's performance on the night of King's death was the most powerful he's ever seen: "It wasn't like a show—it was more like a funeral, a wake. I think the band was playing more for themselves, for their own feelings, rather than for an audience. It was like we were sitting in on something very personal." Spann, the pianist, would later record an aching dirge, "Blues for Martin Luther King," inspired by the communal grief of that night.

After the show, a young Tea Party employee named Ravi was assaulted in the middle of the night as he rode his motorcycle home to Roxbury. As his attackers descended upon him, one of the assailants yelled that he recognized the boy from the Tea Party. It probably saved his life, says Nelson, who remembers the boy coming to work the next day with his head "grotesquely swollen."

Overnight, dozens were arrested, primarily in the Grove Hall and Blue Hill Avenue sections of Roxbury. Burglar alarms rang out from smashed storefronts as groups of young men traveled in packs, throwing stones. Meanwhile, government employees and community activists were galvanized into action. "I remember drifting down to City Hall knowing that we'd have to do something, not knowing what that would be," says Kay Gibbs, who was then an assistant to Tom Atkins, Boston's first black city councilor. Though she was working for the government, Gibbs considered herself something of a radical at the time. "Our eyes were on Stokely and SNCC," the rapidly radicalizing Student Nonviolent Coordinating Committee, she recalls. "The fact that even an accommodationist could be killed, that was too much to take. It was like, 'If they'd kill him, they'd kill anybody.' "

In Roxbury, where activists had been hard at work in early 1968 on demands for reform, Chuck Turner was in a meeting when he heard the news about King's death. Turner had known Stokely Carmichael since the former's days as a reporter in Washington, D.C., earlier in the decade. During Carmichael's visit to Boston in December 1967, the outgoing SNCC leader had warned community leaders about the mounting potential for a government crackdown on black radicals. The warning vitalized the city's civil rights organizers. Within weeks, Turner had been named co-chair of the new Boston Black United Front, a coalition of black advocacy groups, including local chapters of the National Association for the Advancement of Colored People, the Congress of Racial Equality, and the Black Panthers, as well as Mel King's New Urban League of Greater Boston and Ellen Jackson's Operation Exodus, an early facilitator of the school busing initiatives that would tear at the heart of Boston in the coming decade.

"Stokely had come back from a trip through the Far East, and there was the thought that by creating alliances with some of the more conservative forces, that would provide some level of protection," explains Turner, who has served as a Boston city councilor since 1999. The Black United Front was in the process of creating a twenty-one-point set of demands for the city of Boston, including the clause that attracted the bulk of the media attention—a call for the rejection of white-owned businesses in Boston's black neighborhoods. After a series of Sunday morning strategy sessions at the Pewter Pot Muffin House on Boylston Street, there had been a major convocation on the third of April at the Roxbury Multi-Service Center to hammer out the list of demands. The Black United Front was ready to make its petitions public; for these activists, King's brutal murder was definitive proof that there could be no more debate.

In the mayor's office, the primary concern was to address the neighborhoods with sensitivity. The most pressing concern was to keep the city's police officers calm. The rioting that had occurred the previous year after the protest by Mothers for Adequate Welfare was widely perceived to have been avoidable but for the aggressive policing of certain members of the force. The recent problems in Memphis over the sanitation workers' strike, as Harvard Professor Thomas F. Pettigrew told the *Globe*, were "almost as much police-initiated as the riot in Boston last summer. The television showed the police slugging nonviolent bystanders right along with the violent." Kevin White's administration, just completing its first hundred days in office, was determined to elude a similar fiasco. The mayor was eager to comply with Roxbury leaders when they recommended the community be sealed off, to protect it from "curiosity seekers." In fact, his office had been momentarily stymied by one caller requesting one hundred horses for the neighborhood. Amid some confusion, it was determined that the caller was seeking *wooden* horses—police barricades.

Working closely with Police Commissioner Edmund L. McNamara, whom the mayor had unsuccessfully attempted to oust just weeks before, White immediately declared all lines of communication open and encouraged residents to report incidents directly to his office. "I think there was originally a period of shock, a quiet period when no one knew how to react," as White recalled on the afternoon of Friday, the fifth, on the issues program *Backgrounds* on WGBH, which was Boston's public-broadcasting flagship station. "There was a deep sense of loss. But then the emotions set in, and we tried to keep in touch with the community leaders, to find out whether the situation was going to become inflammable." He and his aides, he said, sought to "keep a reaction that's consistent to the principles for which [King] stood—namely, nonviolence and peace." Many have credited Rep. Barney Frank, the longtime House Democrat from Massachusetts who was then executive assistant to the mayor, with helping cooler heads prevail. The mayor, the *Globe* reported, stayed well past midnight—were images of burning Atlanta dancing in his head?—and members of his staff maintained an overnight vigil.

In the morning, when Mayor White and his staff resumed the business of maintaining order in the city, he was presented with a fresh dilemma by the newly elected city councilor Tom Atkins. Atkins, a fast-rising figure in local politics, had just become the first African-American in Boston's history to be elected to city-wide office. Atkins told the mayor he'd just learned that Boston Garden management was about to cancel that night's scheduled performance by the singer James Brown. It was, at the moment, not the sort of crisis on which the mayor was inclined to expend much energy.

But Atkins was adamant. He'd received a call from Jimmy Byrd, a gregarious and very popular disc jockey on Boston's WILD, where Atkins had been a program host for some time. The AM station, which originally featured classical music, was a mixed bag of programming in the 1960s, with ethnic specialty shows catering to the city's Italian, Greek, and Armenian communities. But Byrd, who went by the on-air nickname Early Byrd, was well-known throughout the city as the voice of the station's soul and gospel shows. For years he had worked closely with James Brown's handlers, promoting the singer's regular appearances at the old Boston Arena near Northeastern University and the Hibernian Hall in Roxbury. Now, Brown's people wanted some explanation for the impending cancelation.

Byrd, the DJ, knew instinctively what the politicians might have otherwise overlooked: the city was likely going to have a considerable problem on its hands with fourteen thousand young James Brown fans making their way across town, through the Financial District and the old Brahmin Beacon Hill neighborhood to the all-Italian North End (to which the Garden was adjacent), only to discover that the concert had been canceled.

Under those circumstances, the rioting the city so feared was, Byrd felt, all but assured. Atkins agreed, and he relayed their concern to the mayor, telling him, "People who would not otherwise have been taking part in any unlawful behavior will have an independent reason to be mad at the establishment. And you're it."

Brown's audience already had a reputation for over-the-top exuberance. "What James Brown does to audiences," *Soul* magazine had only recently explained, "has been keenly observed by psychologists. It is a study in inciting mass, frenzied hysteria." In 1968, rock 'n' roll was still widely suspected as an unwelcome infliction by the generations that had grown up to the sweet strains of *Your Hit Parade*. Brown's audiences were especially noted for their delirium; even before Beatlemania, the shrill crowd noise of Brown's *Live at the Apollo* made it clear that his shows were prone to spontaneous combustion. Irwin Pate, a promoter who worked for Brown in those years, recalls a Thanksgiving show in his own city, Buffalo, when hundreds of fans stormed a sold-out auditorium. "They came in through the ticket windows," he says. "The firemen had no control."

In late 1966, the band had headlined Kansas City's Municipal Auditorium, where police shut down the show, according to the singer, on charges of obscenity. In his autobiography, he claimed that the women in his support act, the Jewels, were wearing skimpy shorts that attending officers found inappropriate. Published reports cited heavy drinking in the crowd and a disputed decision in a dance contest as the roots of the fracas. Whatever the cause, more than fifty policemen faced off against unruly concertgoers until hours after the concert's abrupt ending.

And Brown himself had a well-deserved reputation as a hothead. After some had taken to calling Solomon Burke the "King of Soul," Brown once hired Burke as an opening act. Instead of letting him perform, he forced Burke to sit in the wings and watch the real King of Soul slay a Chicago crowd. According to legend, the singer once shot up Club 15, a juke joint on the outskirts of Macon, after a homecoming show at the City Auditorium. One of Brown's fiercest adversaries was Joe Tex, a King labelmate who wrote "Baby, You're Right," an R&B hit for Brown in 1961. When Tex accused Brown of stealing some of his onstage moves, the ruthless singer compounded the insult by stealing Tex's wife, Bea Ford, who became not only a short-lived featured singer for the James Brown Revue, but also the latest of Brown's extramarital girlfriends. Tex, in reply, wrote "You Keep Her." But that wasn't the end of it. On the night of Brown's Macon homecoming, Tex, sharing the bill at Club 15 with Otis Redding's Pinetoppers, mocked the city's man of honor by mimicking Brown's well-traveled cape routine, reportedly entangling himself in a tattered blanket onstage and bawling "Please,

please, please . . . get me out of this cape!" When Brown and his entourage got wind of the clowning, the enraged singer showed up at the club, pulled out a pistol, and fired several rounds in the air. The Pinetoppers' Johnny Jenkins later claimed that several patrons, grazed by stray bullets, were paid hush money in hundred-dollar bills.

In spite of these ominous signs—just how would this mercurial figure handle the onus of performing under such trying circumstances?—the fact of the matter was that by April 1968, James Brown was Soul Brother Number One to black America. Wherever he traveled, his arrival was a major event, a ritual of ostentation and a cathartic release of suppressed emotions.

But if Brown had black America under his thumb, and if the culturally attuned white children of the postwar baby boom were growing hipper to his new bag, he remained largely unrecognized to those outside the sphere of pop music. When the issue of the Boston Garden concert first came up in the mayor's office, White thought the headliner in question was *Jim* Brown, the all-star running back.

From the start, the dialogue between the mayor and Atkins was volatile. White had no intention of reversing the decision to cancel; Atkins thought the mayor's position was "crazy." It was not the first time the two men had disagreed. There were policy differences, and clashing political egos.

Atkins had been raised in the Midwest, about a hundred miles east of Chicago in Elkhart, Indiana, the working-class home of industries ranging from musical instruments and mobile homes to Alka-Seltzer. After attending Harvard, where, in a thesis paper, he criticized the NAACP's cautious approach, he began a lifelong commitment to civil rights by accepting a challenge to go to work for the organization's local chapter. In Boston, his aggressive approach put him on a collision course with White, who was, for many, the embodiment of the typical Boston Irish view toward the black population.

After several acerbic discussions, the two parties had a breakthrough. What if the concert were to be televised locally? That way, the fourteen thousand or so who might be diverted by the show could be magically transformed into a captive audience of hundreds of thousands. (While Byrd claims he was the first to come up with the solution, the idea is generally credited to Barney Frank, though the congressman today can't quite recall.) This, to Atkins, sounded like a promising gesture. White was finally realizing that Brown could be an asset in keeping the peace.

Other city officials were asked to weigh in. Among them was Paul Parks, a Boston-based engineer and activist who had just, in late March, been awarded directorship of the first Model Cities program approved by the Johnson administration—a "human renewal" program to augment Boston's controversial urban renewal project of the period. Parks, who was then chairman of the NAACP's Education Committee, had extensive experience on voter-registration drives in the Deep South with Andy Young, who had introduced him to Dr. King. The meeting in the mayor's office was attended by Barney Frank, Tom Atkins, Police Commissioner McNamara, and Superintendent Bill Bradley, among others. Together they convinced the mayor that the concert would have a healing effect on the city.

So Kevin White forged ahead with the plan to televise. During the 1960s the city of Boston relied heavily on the guidance of a board of Brahmin businessmen officially called the Coordinating Committee, but casually known as the "Vault." Since 1959, institutional executives such as Ralph Lowell of the Boston Safe Deposit and Trust Company and Gerald Blakely, Jr., of Cabot, Cabot and Forbes had served as a civic steering committee, working with the mayoral administrations of John Hynes, John Collins, and now Kevin White to address the city's economic, developmental, and cultural growing pains. The group's informal name grew out of the fact that they conducted their meetings in a boardroom behind a massive vaulted door inside the Safe Deposit building.

Lowell, often called "Mr. Boston" for his lifelong dedication to the well-being of his native city, was the founding father of WGBH. The station and its radio affiliate were electronic extensions of the prestigious Lowell family's century-old commitment to public education in Boston. Lowell's ancestor, John Lowell, Jr., an heir to the family fortune amassed from the manufacture of production machinery for the textile industry, served in the Massachusetts State Senate in the 1820s. After the consecutive deaths of his wife and two children, John Lowell consoled himself by traveling the world. Before leaving Boston, he authorized a will that left a sizeable portion of his estate for the foundation of the Lowell Institute, which called for the establishment of an ongoing public lecture series for the senator's city, the "Athens of America." More than a hundred years later, with interest in the lecture series waning, the institute formed the Cooperative Broadcasting Council with six of Boston's most prominent colleges to present the Lowell lectures on local television.

The rejuvenation of the lecture series led Ralph Lowell to establish his own station, WGBH, in 1955. (While the call letters were chosen to signify Great Blue Hill, the peak in Milton,

Massachusetts, just south of Boston, where the original transmitter was located, some joked that they stood for "God Bless Harvard.") From its inception, the station was deeply invested in the Lowell family's belief in lifelong learning, developing new programming such as events with the Boston Symphony and Arthur Fiedler's Boston Pops, as well as Eleanor Roosevelt's interview series, *Prospects of Mankind*. In the early 1960s, the station turned to the looming issue of race relations, premiering a civil rights–themed program called *For Freedom Now*.

Given the city's close relationship with Lowell and his colleagues at the Vault, when the idea of televising the concert arose, WGBH was the logical destination. In the afternoon White approached Hartford Gunn, the station manager, who was two years removed from heading to Washington to become the first president of the Public Broadcasting Service. "I got his call just after 3:30, only five hours before Brown was scheduled to go on," Gunn recalled. "I said we'd televise the show even before I knew whether we could really manage it."

There was, however, another problem. James Brown was still in New York, where he was wrapping up his work on the *Man to Man* special before jetting up to Boston. And he was unreachable. Jimmy Byrd had been in close contact with Greg Moses, Brown's business manager, but now Moses was unavailable, too. The producers at WGBH were pressing for an answer. Every minute was critical—they now had a matter of hours to set up a broadcast for which they typically would have required days. Atkins, in a panic, asked Byrd whether he thought Brown would agree to the broadcast. "I don't think he'll mind," the DJ replied.

The mayor's office quickly organized a press conference. At

WILD, which had switched to a temporary all-gospel format, Byrd arranged for public service announcements explaining that the show would be televised. Then he took the station's sound truck through the streets of Boston's black neighborhoods to deliver the news. Across the country his colleagues in radio were addressing their listeners with unprecedented urgency; as one DJ would recall, "Black radio came of age the night Martin Luther King was killed."

At WGBH, which had been scheduled to broadcast Laurence Olivier's stage production of *Uncle Vanya* at 8:30, Russ Morash was immediately tapped as the producer of the live remote. Morash would later be responsible for the development of some of PBS's most iconic programming, including *The French Chef* and *This Old House*. Yet in 1968 Morash was, by his own admission, still a "young punk." Another youthful staffer, David Atwood, quickly convinced Morash to let him direct the concert feed. They were both accustomed to producing live programming featuring many of Boston's high-minded institutions, ranging from specials at the Museum of Fine Arts and the Boston Pops to political discussion.

The station had just acquired a new mobile unit in an unmarked tractor-trailer, which was hastily relocated to the Boston Garden. Although the station had begun using color cameras the previous year, there was no time to lay color cables. Instead, the crew was obliged to use the existing black-and-white cables permanently installed in the old Garden for broadcasts of Bruins and Celtics games.

Forty years old in 1968, the Garden was already showing signs of wear. Following the lead of New York's Madison Square Garden, the building had been part of a master plan by the promoter and developer Tex Rickard, who dreamed of constructing a half-dozen big-city "Gardens" for major entertainment and sporting events. Rickard's grand designs fell short when he died of complications from an appendectomy in 1929. Walter Brown was named general manager of the Boston Garden in 1937; eventually, he would assume the facility's presidency, as well as ownership of the National Basketball Association's Boston Celtics and the National Hockey League's Boston Bruins, both of which played home games in the building. Over the years the venue, famous for its parquet basketball floor (relocated from the crosstown Boston Arena in the 1950s), hosted many of Boston's most notable events. The flamboyant wrestler "Gorgeous" George Wagner was a regular attraction; in 1954 Liberace celebrated his first arena show by signing autographs at the Garden until three in the morning.

The Celtics, the NBA's dominant organization in the 1960s, were due to play the Philadelphia 76ers in the first game of the league's Eastern Division finals on Friday, April 5, in Philadelphia. Before leaving on an afternoon flight, Bill Russell, the great Celtics center who had been appointed the league's first black coach in 1967, conferred with his friend and on-court rival, Wilt Chamberlain, and the two teams agreed to postpone their second game, planned for the Garden on Sunday. With such short notice for a postponement, however, game one would take place as scheduled. (The issue was an important one for the basketball players, who were well aware of the criticism the National Football League had received when it decided not to postpone its games following the assassination of President Kennedy in 1963.) En route early Friday afternoon to an emergency meeting at the Garden with Celtics general manager Red

Auerbach, several of the team's players were caught in traffic near Post Office Square as thousands of Bostonians marched from the Boston Common to the old Federal Building to memorialize King's murder.

At the Garden, Atwood, Morash, and their colleagues were operating in familiar territory, having worked on broadcasts of college hockey games there. "The old Garden was great," says Atwood. "It had a wonderful intimacy. You could smell the people." Rickard had designed the blocky building for boxing, the country's most lucrative spectator sport in the 1920s. Every fan, he decreed, should be close enough to see "the sweat of the boxers' brows." As a result, the distance between spectators and performers was considerably less than in most comparably sized arenas. The compact scale contributed to a distinct home-court advantage for the city's professional athletes, but it also meant that hostile situations were impossible to ignore.

While the crew prepared the concert feed, James Brown arrived in Boston, landing at Logan Airport in his Lear jet, with its powder-blue interior and the letters "JB" emblazoned on the tail. Atkins met the singer at the airport in the city's executive limousine, a peace offering he'd cajoled out of the mayor. Despite the dignitary's reception, Brown was angry. The show couldn't be televised, he said. He was contractually obligated to a noncompete clause in his syndication deal for *Man to Man*, which was set to air in various markets over the next few months. On the drive through the Sumner Tunnel to the Garden, he told Atkins, "Brother, I'd love to be of help. My lawyers are telling me I'm stuck."

For Brown, the situation grew more discouraging when the car pulled up at the Garden, where fans by the score were arranging refunds for their tickets. As in so many cities across the country, authorities in Boston had recommended that citizens stay home that evening. Now that they would be able to watch the show in the safety of their own living rooms, many ticketholders were heeding the advice and turning in their tickets. This, for Brown, was an outrage. The city was killing his gate. He feared he would be playing to an empty house, and that those who turned in their tickets for refunds would blame him when they were unable to see the concert on television. The situation, he felt, could bring real trouble.

Inside the Garden's administrative offices, various members of Brown's band and entourage, who had arrived in the city earlier in the day, milled around, awaiting the arrival of the boss. Though they spoke in hushed tones about the King assassination, the looming issue was the arrival of a very angry bull of a man named James Brown. The band members had no more answers than the television crew. Someone asked for James Brown's representative, and a member of the group replied, "He's not here yet. James Brown is James Brown's representative."

When Brown strode in, draped in a white cashmere coat, he greeted his musicians. Looking around for someone from the television station, he pulled aside Al Potter, WGBH's program director. Potter confirmed the plans to broadcast, and he listened as the singer explained his contractual obligation. To Potter, it sounded like a reasonable explanation.

By this point, Brown was sufficiently muddled. If he went on TV, he was setting himself up to be sued. If he didn't, the city's sour mood could be turned in his direction. Either way, he was about to take a bath on the concert gross. The mayor's office was out of solutions; no one wanted to talk to Brown.

So Atkins sat down with Brown again and took it upon himself to broker a deal. The singer pledged to try to secure a release from the exclusive provision of his contract. In exchange, Atkins suggested that he could get the city to cover the losses Brown would incur from the quickly dwindling gate. Atkins called the mayor, who was hunkered down at City Hall, to recommend that the city guarantee the difference between the final receipts and the ticket proceeds that would have accompanied a sold-out house. Once again, he and White were at odds. If word got out that the city had agreed to pay tens of thousands of dollars to an entertainer, White sputtered, his political career would be over. Atkins argued otherwise: if James Brown refused to perform in a dispute over money, "people all over the city—particularly Roxbury, Dorchester [and] the South End—will know that you canceled or otherwise killed this concert." Atkins didn't care where the money came from, but he was insistent about its necessity.

Just months before, White had been elected as the candidate most likely to address Boston's growing racial strife with sensitivity. In fact, the city's anti-integrationists had begun calling him "Mayor Black." But Kevin White was also duly noted for his lofty ambitions, and there was mounting concern that his appeasement of Boston's African-American population was mere grandstanding. Upon taking office White had earned immediate comparisons with John Lindsay, New York's trim, photogenic mayor, and Boston's new mayor was being discussed, however prematurely, as a potential candidate on the national level. Now Atkins told him that if Boston rioted over this, he wouldn't be taken seriously anywhere.

Hinting that the city could expect to be sued by the entertainer for interfering with his contract with the Garden, Atkins eventually wrested from Kevin White a grudging okay for the box-office guarantee. Brown later praised Atkins for amending the situation. "I would have gone on and done the show anyway and taken the losses," he claimed, "but by then I thought the city ought to do *something* right."

It was about a quarter to seven. The concert was set to begin at eight. With the mayor now in the building, Paul Parks and other local leaders worked the incoming crowd, communicating with City Hall by walkie-talkie, attempting to ensure that the concert would take place without incident. As groups of fans began arriving for the show, Parks engaged them in conversation about Dr. King's death, and he urged them to honor the minister's legacy of nonviolence that night.

One delegation of fans was ushered up to meet with Brown, who made his own appeal for restraint. "He said it didn't make any sense having them in there hurting each other," says Parks. "And they heard him. He had a large hand in keeping that crowd at ease. . . . He handled those kids beautifully."

★ ★ ★ 4 ★ ★ ★

BRING IT UP

"The beating of drums, the blowing of horns and trumpets, and shouting of men . . ." The writer is Charles Dickens, setting the stage for a rowdy political rally in his debut novel, *The Posthumous Papers of the Pickwick Club*, better known as *The Pickwick Papers*. In *Pickwick*, the London musical adaptation of Dickens's story, the lead character distills his worldview into the show's signature song, "If I Ruled the World," with lyrics written by Leslie Bricusse. Though the play flopped in its transition onto Broadway in 1965, it inspired a hit version of the song by Tony Bennett and another by Sammy Davis, Jr.

That's how it came to James Brown, who carried a not-so-secret longing to establish himself as a casino-style showman on par with Bennett, Frank Sinatra, Bobby Darin, and other assiduously "cool" pop crooners, even as he was running hot with the invention of funk. No one had a feel for music—any music—like James Brown did, and by the late 1960s he saw the lounge singers as rival businessmen defining another market into which he could expand.

Brown began his show at the Boston Garden as he did many gigs around the time, with his own uncharacteristically subdued version of "If I Ruled the World." Before he emerged from the wings, his band warmed up the sparse crowd—between two and three thousand, by all accounts, given the dire warnings on the streets—with its usual introductory medley. The walk-up music began with a soft-touch rendition of "Groovin'," the recent, day-dreamy number-one pop hit by the Rascals. Utterly ignoring the trying circumstances, the toodling music was almost defiantly nonchalant. The seventeen-piece band onstage included Pee Wee Ellis, Maceo Parker, Joe Dupars, Waymon Reed, St. Clair Pinckney, Levi Raspbury, and newcomer Fred Wesley in the brass section; another newcomer, bassist Tim Drummond—the first white musician to join the band, lately of Cincinnati's Dapps, the club band that had backed Brown on his recent studio session for "I Can't Stand Myself"; dual drummers Clyde Stubblefield and Nate Jones; Jimmy Nolen and Alfonso "Country" Kellum on guitars; featured singers Bobby Byrd and Marva Whitney; and a trio of violinists.

Little about the show had changed from recent weeks, yet for one night, every song would be fraught with an unintentional new layer of meaning. With the sole spotlight at center stage and much of the huge band hidden in shadows to viewers at home, Brown suddenly slipped up to the microphone in a natty white three-piece suit and a cream-colored turtleneck and began, quietly, to sing.

"If I ruled the world," he purred, "every day would be like the first day of spring." In fact, it was cool and wet outside; many in the Garden crowd were wearing trenchcoats. If the maudlin lyrics to this show tune weren't nearly as eloquent as even the most casual of Dr. King's remarks, they nevertheless rose to the occasion. If it were up to him, he promised, every man (it was, after all, a man's man's man's world) would be as free as a bird. As he always did, Brown bit off the word free, delivering it in boldface. That lone syllable—*free*—stood apart as an emphatic demand, not just another strand of melody.

Unlike Samuel Pickwick, who came by his political consideration accidentally, Brown was already attuned to the art of campaigning, seasoned as he was with the self-dramatizing rhetoric of creating a public persona. For him, "If I Ruled the World" was no mere pipe dream. By early 1968, he had begun to see himself as a freedom fighter with a unique authority. When the song concluded, however, and it came time to speak his customary welcome to the audience, it was apparent that even Brown was unsure just what could possibly be said, given the awful circumstances. After thanking the audience for their support, he told them, as he did at every show, that he owed them his success.

"I want you to know that I'm still a soul brother," he said. "You've made it possible for me to be a first-class man in all respects." Instinctively, he began to ease into his familiar sermonic set-piece, talking about his radio stations, how he had shined shoes outside of WRDW in Augusta as a boy, making three cents a pair, then five. "Finally got up to six cents," he said. "But now I own that station. You know what that is? *That's* black power. This is the way you do it."

*　　　*　　　*

"**I**'m a model man," James Brown once said, and he took the assignment with utmost sincerity. He felt he could "even out a lot of the faults in society" by the examples he set. In fact, this man, one of the most farsighted musical minds of the modern world, was in some ways a bit of a cultural relic. During Brown's lifetime, the notion of the role model all but vanished in America. Scandal, corruption, and the new transparency of the media age have all contributed to the demise of the traditional American hero. But Brown believed himself to be, and never ceased to present himself as, a paragon.

He liked to think of himself as a child of the world, and he claimed a virtual melting pot of race and ethnicity. His mother's father, he suggested, was "highly Asian." His maternal great-grandmother—"almost a full-blooded American Indian"—had hair "so long she could sit on it," and he had a paternal grandfather who was also, he said, Native American, perhaps Cherokee. Whatever the particulars, his ancestry was decidedly mixed—"maybe a little Egyptian King Tut thrown in for good measure," as he once suggested. "Because of all these different bloodlines," he would claim, "I feel a connection to everybody, not to any special race, but to the human race." Always the self-promoter, his instinct was never to limit his market.

Even the incomparables owe some of their singularity to the impressions they take. Brown was fond of claiming descendance from Geronimo, the Apache leader who was one of the last holdouts against United States sovereignty over the American West. Having Native American blood, he could lay claim to his home soil in a way that the pure descendants of African slaves could not. He could declare himself a devout countryman, yet identify with a warrior who resisted the United

States government. In this way he could reconcile his staunch patriotism with his equally passionate advocacy of black independence. Brown, an avid fan of Western films and comic books as a kid, was undoubtedly aware from a young age of the Geronimo legacy.

His mind, as he often noted, was likewise fired by the adventures of Hopalong Cassidy, the fictional clean-living, black-clad cowboy played by William Boyd and featured in dozens of serial motion pictures in the 1930s and '40s. (Brown's fascination with Hopalong Cassidy was shared by another notably self-made figure, F. Scott Fitzgerald's Jay Gatsby, who keeps a self-improvement schedule on a back page of his copy of an original Hoppy novel.) "Black kids have nothing," Brown once told an interviewer. While white kids can look up to beloved presidents, Lincoln or Kennedy, he recalled, "I had Superman and Hopalong Cassidy."

The details of his upbringing, however sparse, have been retold countless times, and have come to sound like an especially harsh—and wholly American—fairy tale. The only child of Joseph Gardner Brown and Susie Behling, James Joseph Brown claimed to have been stillborn at birth, only to be revived, aptly enough, wailing. When he was a boy, his mother abandoned the family in their tumbledown shack in the woods near Barnwell, South Carolina. Joe Brown, an itinerant who often labored in turpentine camps, extracting resin from pine trees, a grueling occupation offset by stints on farms or as a hired hand in filling stations, was soon obliged to leave his only son with relatives across the state line in Augusta. The slums of Augusta and the city's surrounding area, sometimes called Georgialina, were deeply fixed in Brown's blood. It would have been "inconceivable for James Brown to be born and raised in, say, Massachusetts," the singer would explain.

James's aunt Minnie, actually a great-aunt who had been present at his eventful birth, took him to live with another aunt named Handsome Washington, whom everyone called Honey. Honey's house in the "Terry" was home to a large number of wayward men, women, and children, with gambling, moonshine, and prostitution the main sources of income. For Brown, Augusta was "sin city," but it was also a place where he had friends and surrogate family and was looked after, unlike his earliest years in South Carolina. In his autobiography, he recalled long stretches spent alone as an adolescent in the piney woods. Such isolation "worked a change in me that stayed with me from then on," he would write. "It gave me my own mind."

Brown's birthdate has been the subject of some debate. In the early years of his career, it was often given as May 3, 1928. Most sources, however, agree that he was born in 1933; when Brown died in 2006, virtually every obituary across the globe gave his age as seventy-three. Jack Bart, the singer's booking agent for decades after succeeding his father, Ben Bart, the Colonel Tom Parker figure in Brown's early career, recounts a tale of the singer befriending a woman working in the United States Passport Bureau, and suggests it's possible his client could have arranged a revised date of birth. But Alan Leeds, Brown's onetime tour manager and an acknowledged Brown historian who has written extensively about his former employer, says the 1928 birth year may have been mistakenly pulled from biographical material on another musician named James Brown.

Whatever his precise age, Brown's career bridged some of the oldest forms of American popular entertainment to the dominant sounds of the new millennium. His formidable dancing was an intuitive amalgam of steps, slides, and stomps dating all the way back to the earliest days of vaudeville and minstrelsy. The first songs he sang in the woods when his father bought him a ten-cent harmonica, he would recall, included Stephen Foster's "Oh! Susanna" and the traditional "John Henry."

Physically, Brown's dazzling stage presence almost singlehandedly ensured that old-fashioned showmanship would remain a critical component of popular music well into the digital age. "James Brown is my greatest inspiration," said Michael Jackson at Brown's 2006 funeral service in Augusta. Brown often attributed his movement to the buck dancing he did on the streets of Augusta as a youth. In addition to shining shoes, delivering ice, running errands, and corraling johns for Aunt Honey's stable of girls, he often made tip money by entertaining the soldiers stationed at nearby Fort Gordon during World War II. Having learned a few rudimentary steps from a cousin, Willie Glenn, who also lived at Honey's house (Glenn, who remained a close companion to Brown for the rest of the singer's life, was then Big Junior to Brown's Little Junior), the young man recognized that there were quarters to be pried from servicemen seeking some relief from the tedium of military training.

Buck dancing, with roots in Irish clogs and jigs and slave-ship dances ordered by captains—the term is a derivative of *buccaneer*—was a common element of minstrelsy at least as far back as the 1830s. Its most famous practitioner, William Henry Lane, a free Negro reportedly born in Providence, Rhode Island, in 1825, performed celebrated buck dances under the stage name Master Juba. His prowess in competition led to a starring role in the otherwise all-white revue called the Ethiopian Minstrels, where he was billed as "The Greatest Dancer in the World." Dickens, on a visit to Manhattan's notorious Five Points neighborhood, reported that here was a truly prodigious talent: "Single shuffle, double shuffle, cut and cross-cut; snapping his fingers, rolling his eyes, turning in his knees, presenting the backs of his legs in front, spinning about on his toes and heels like nothing but the man's fingers on the tambourine; dancing with two left legs, two right legs, two wooden legs, two wire legs, two spring legs—all sorts of legs and no legs." The description, and the "Greatest Dancer" billing, might have come from James Brown's own supercharged performance on *The T.A.M.I. Show* in 1964. But buck dancing was already considered passe by the 1920s, when more sophisticated dance steps—tap, the Charleston, the Lindy Hop—ruled the dance halls.

Like boys of any generation, Brown had an idea that he might become a star in one of his favorite sports. His local reputation for an almost maniacal toughness was enhanced when he continued to play football after breaking a leg. The cast he wore earned him a new nickname, "Crip." But baseball and boxing were his two real loves. "I was much better at baseball than singing," he claimed, and his nimble hook slides on the base paths would become a comic centerpiece of his early stage show. A stocky left-handed pitcher, by his own account he featured a lively fastball, a good curveball, and a deceptive knuckleball. The Detroit Tigers held spring training in Augusta and were affiliated with a farm team there. The Hall of Fame career of Ty Cobb, a longtime resident of the city who began playing professionally with the Augusta Tourists in 1904, was well-known to Brown and his young friends. It's tempting to speculate that Brown gleaned some of his own athletic tenacity from hearing tales about Cobb in his heyday, a self-proclaimed "snarling wild-cat" (and notorious bigot) who had the nickname "The Georgia Peach" decades before it was bestowed upon the rock 'n' roll shouter Little Richard.

As a boxer, Brown's hero was unquestionably Beau Jack, a lightweight titleholder of the 1940s and another product of Augusta. Jack, born Sidney Walker, made his name as a competitor in the brutal battles royal of his hometown, in which groups of six young fighters were pitted against each other in a blind-folded free-for-all, with the last man standing declared the winner. Through the patronage of golf star Bobby Jones (yet another Augustan), Jack was sent to western Massachusetts for training. His agility and superior punching ability eventually made him a prime attraction at Madison Square Garden, where he staged a legendary four-fight series with fellow lightweight Bob Montgomery, the "Philadelphia Bobcat." Jack's twenty-one appearances in main-event bouts at the Garden remain a record. Brown was a devoted fan, listening intently to radio broadcasts of many of those fights.

Like his hero, Brown participated in several battles royal in Augusta. Despite the fact that the fighters were typically black boys and the organizers white men, he saw the practice as "comedy. I'd be out there stumbling around, swinging wild, and hearing the people *laughing*. I didn't know I was being exploited; all I knew was that I was getting paid a dollar and having fun." If the young James Brown was not yet savvy enough to recognize exploitation when he saw it, the author Ralph Ellison certainly did, in the disturbing battle-royal vignette that set the stage for his great novel, *Invisible Man*. "Blindfolded, I could no longer control my motions," explains Ellison's unnamed narrator. "I had no dignity. I stumbled about like a baby or a drunken man. The smoke had become thicker and with each new blow it seemed to sear and further restrict my lungs. My saliva became like hot bitter glue. A glove connected with my head, filling my mouth with warm blood. It was everywhere." As the fight wears on, the boy becomes delirious. "I trembled with excitement, forgetting my pain. I would get the gold and the bills, I thought. I would use both hands. I would throw my body against the boys nearest me to block them from the gold."

It was hardly an auspicious beginning for Brown. Life on the streets, with no parental presence and precious little guidance, inevitably led to petty crime. But when Brown was sentenced, at age fifteen, to eight to sixteen years in reform school for taking clothing from parked cars, he told Willie Glenn not to worry. "When I get out of here," he said, echoing something he'd often heard from Aunt Honey, "the *world* is going to know about me."

By this time he had an inkling that music, not sports, might be his salvation. (As Motown founder Berry Gordy, another onetime boxing hopeful, once explained, his own career path became apparent when he came across two posters in a gym, one advertising an upcoming fight, the other a "Battle of the Bands" between Duke Ellington and Stan Kenton. "The fighters were about twenty-three and looked fifty," Gordy recalled, and "the band leaders about fifty and looked twenty-three.") Brown had been singing the spirituals he heard in church with his cousin and other young men around the neighborhood. He met a man with a drum kit and learned the rudiments of keeping time; the son of a liquor-store owner for whom he made deliveries taught him some chording on an upright piano.

Brown also claimed that he was introduced to bottleneck-style guitar playing by the onetime recording artist Tampa Red, who, according to the singer, had a girlfriend at Aunt Honey's. Born Hudson Woodbridge, and better known as Hudson Whittaker, Tampa Red was probably best recognized for teaming with Ma Rainey on the bawdy blues "It's Tight Like That." For many years he was partnered with the barrelhouse pianist Thomas A. Dorsey, otherwise known as Georgia Tom. While their collaborations were typically rich with innuendo, Dorsey, the son of a minister, grew into a notable alternate career as "the father of gospel music." His standard, "Take My Hand, Precious Lord," written in grief over the death in childbirth of his first wife, Nettie, was a favorite of Martin Luther King, Jr. (Elvis Presley, meanwhile, was partial to Dorsey's "Peace in the Valley.")

Brown's interaction with Tampa Red was presumably minimal; no chronicle, including his own autobiography, gives their acquaintance more than a passing mention. But if he did receive some tutoring from the bluesman, it is not difficult to trace the potential influences. Although Brown reiterated that he was not predisposed toward Red's brand of music—of the blues, he wrote, "I'd *sing* 'em sometimes, but I still didn't *like* 'em," in part because they reminded him of the songs his father sang while toiling in the turpentine camps—Tampa Red often played a mischievous, upbeat style of the blues that was marketed as "hokum." If the sexually charged music that became Brown's specialty in the heyday of funk—"Get Up (I Feel Like Being a) Sex Machine"—had predecessors, they would certainly include examples of the so-called "copulatin' blues" such as "It's Tight Like That." Red was also a showman, with years of theater experience that gave him a reputation as one of the more urbane bluesmen. No hillbilly, he made a habit of slyly alluding to the black experience in his music, recording songs with titles such as "Black Hearted Blues" and "Too Black Bad."

As for contemporary artists Brown would have heard on the radio as he approached young adulthood, he took incentive from the raucous voices of the 1940s jump bandleaders—rock 'n' roll forebears such as Wynonie Harris and Roy Brown—as well as good-time orchestra conductors Count Basie and Buddy Johnson and the blues shouters Big Joe Turner and Willie Mae "Big Mama" Thornton. The "hi-de-ho" man Cab Calloway, who asked a nation of zoot-suiters "Are You Hep to the Jive?," doubtlessly inspired Brown's fashion and phraseology. But Brown was particularly infatuated with Louis Jordan, the king of 1940s rhythm and blues and one of the most influential, if underacknowledged, architects of the rock 'n' roll sound.

As a young teenager Jordan, the son of a musician, left home to travel with Ma and Pa Rainey's Rabbit Foot Minstrels. His recording debut came as the featured singer on Clarence Williams and His Washboard Band's 1934 tune "I Can't Dance, I Got Ants in My Pants." (The phrase is echoed on Brown's own 1973 single "I Got Ants in My Pants, Pt. 1.") In the mid-1930s, Jordan joined Chick Webb's Savoy Ballroom Orchestra a few months ahead of the young bebop singer Ella Fitzgerald, playing alto saxophone, taking vocal turns, and providing comic introductions. The Savoy was then in the midst of jitterbug fever, making for an exuberant atmosphere that fed Jordan's natural instinct for joyful, leave-your-troubles-at-the-doorstep theatricality.

By the late 1930s Jordan had set out on his own. His Tympany Five, actually comprised of six members, specialized in a high-energy distillation of big-band swing, with guitarist Carl Hogan taking a prominent rhythmic role. By the end of World War II, Jordan's merry rhyming and hipster patter were ideally suited to an exhaling, newly optimistic nation, and the bandleader ended 1946 as the second-biggest-selling artist of the year, behind only his occasional collaborator Bing Crosby.

Best known for his comic depictions of the lively neighborhoods where the majority of his audience lived—"Saturday Night Fish Fry," "Ain't Nobody Here But Us Chickens," "Beans and Cornbread"—Jordan "was the first recording artist to project life and situations of the black community on records with humor and dignity," as Sammy Davis, Jr., once said. Jordan's tremendous crossover success was due in part to his innovative short films, primitive music videos that brought the bug-eyed mugging and finger-snapping elation of his stage act to movie theaters across the country, including Augusta's Lenox Theater. Brown's own philosophy of musical escapism clearly traces to the relentless beatitude of his favorite role model. "When you come out to hear me, I want to make you happy," Jordan once said. "I hardly ever do any sad tunes or any tunes that would suggest that you cry."

One live attraction that excited the young Brown was *Silas Green from New Orleans*, a nationally renowned traveling tent show founded in the early 1900s and carried on until mid-century. The show was originally produced by Ephraim Williams, a one-time Wisconsin shoeshine boy turned entertainment pioneer and the only African-American circus owner in the country in the final years of the nineteenth century. When his circus ran into financial trouble, Williams acquired the rights to a vaudeville stage show, also called *Silas Green from New Orleans*, from playwright Salem Tutt Whitney. The event, featuring singing, dancing, comedy, and specialty acts, was loosely framed around the adventures of "short, coal-black" Silas Green, as *Time* magazine noted in 1940, and "tall, tannish" Lilas Bean. The touring company, Prof. Eph Williams's Famous Troubadours, typically carried a band with as many as sixteen pieces, an equally large group of chorus dancers, and some well-known headlining talent, including, at various points, the blues singers Bessie Smith and Willie Mae Thornton. Featuring slapstick gags such as a man passing out over the smell of a putrid old shoe, the show, *Time* reported, "gets broad at times, but never really dirty." Owner Charles Collier, who took over following Williams's death in the 1930s, was apparently patriarchal toward his troupe of seventy-six, watching over "their morals" on the road.

Despite the archaic minstrelsy of the show, *Silas Green* was an early example of a black amusement that could support a social agenda. "If the show has any trouble with whites," who made up roughly one-quarter of its audiences, said *Time*, "it never plays that town again." A big, brassy band, a carnivalesque commitment to pageantry, and well-worn comedy routines, packaged in a diversion popular enough to bring economic leverage to every waystation on the itinerary: the periodic appearance of *Silas Green from New Orleans* in the Augusta of James Brown's youth gave him the entire template for his future revue.

He found another aspect of his future showmanship in the personal magnetism of Bishop Charles Manuel "Sweet Daddy" Grace. As a boy, the singer often joined the residents of the Terry in welcoming the bishop on his intermittent visits. The founder of a church known as the United House of Prayer for All People, Daddy Grace was a legendarily charismatic figure born in 1884 in the Cape Verde Islands. He established his first Apostolic church in southeastern Massachusetts sometime around 1919. A demonstrative preacher with a Daliesque mustache who prompted members of his congregation to speak in tongues, Grace baptized his followers with fire hoses, often accompanied by multiple bands "to assure jumping dance music." The Bishop made extravagant claims, insisting, for instance, that he single-handedly stopped the war with Japan in 1945 on an overnight mission. He dressed flamboyantly, in capes, hand-painted ties, and "lush fabrics" with "gold piping or shiny buttons," and he traveled luxuriously, in Packards and Pierce-Arrows, with a large coterie including chauffeurs, bodyguards, and secretaries. When he died in 1960, *Ebony* magazine called him "a brown-skinned P.T. Barnum who cracked the whip in a circus of gaudy costumes, wildly gyrating acrobats and brass bands that played as if God were a Cosmic Hipster."

In Augusta, Daddy Grace's House of Prayer was located on Wrightsboro Road in the Terry. Though the barnlike building had a dirt floor, members of the congregation (one of the largest in Grace's domain) took pride in the facility, decorating it with colored crepe paper. Over the door hung a sign that read, GREAT JOY! COME TO THE HOUSE OF PRAYER AND FORGET YOUR TROUBLES. Two splinter groups formed similar churches in the Terry, demonstrating, as the bishop's biographer notes, that "even those who did not agree with Grace learned something valuable from him about organization and independence." Grace's appeal must have been extraordinary to the impressionable young Brown, who exulted in the carnival-style parades over which the caped crusader—sometimes called the "Black Christ"—would preside. "He was like a god on earth," Brown would recall. "He had long curly hair, and real long fingernails, and suits made out of money."

Trying out for himself a combination of the preacherly pa-
nache he'd seen in church and the rambunctiousness of the traveling tent shows, Brown began entering amateur-night contests
at the Lenox. He soon won several, singing Hit Parade songs
such as "So Long," which he likely learned from a popular 1940
version by the Cincinnati vocal group the Charioteers. With
his newfound success as a performer, the young Brown formed
a short-lived vocal group called the Cremona Trio, named, perhaps, after the the historic northern Italian city that was part
of the first Roman military outpost. Like Jordan's Tympany Five,
the Trio kept its name even after expanding to five members.
During this period, Brown wrote his first song, which he called
"Goin' Back to Rome." "Rome" for him was Rome, Georgia, on
the opposite side of the state from Augusta. He'd never actually
made that trip—let alone traveled to Italy.

In 1949, Brown got his chance to "go back to" the Rome he'd
never seen, when he was sent to the Georgia Juvenile Training
Institute in Rome to serve time for his arrest on four counts
of breaking and entering and larceny. In the detention center,
he was called "Music Box" for his ability to mimic any style of
music he heard on the radio. He also met a new friend, fellow
inmate Johnny Terry, who would later become one of his original bandmates. Brown appealed to the guards to let him play the
prison's piano, and he and Terry put together a gospel group.

For Brown, the more emotive the sound, the better. His style
of gospel singing was inspired by bawling lead men such as Julius
"June" Cheeks of the Sensational Nightingales, Archie Brownlee of the Original Five Blind Boys of Mississippi, and Rebert H.
(R.H.) Harris, the influential second-generation member of the
long-running Soul Stirrers, the group that had just welcomed a

young Sam Cooke into the fold. Each of these men made their names as gospel innovators by pushing the music to ecstatic peaks of sandpapery righteousness, often working in the style known as the "shout song" or "chop jubilee," featuring racing tempos and coarse, staccato barking and growling. Brownlee, who died prematurely in 1960, has been called the "hardest singing" voice in gospel.

Gospel was Brown's tunnel out of juvie. After submitting a petition for early release and telling the warden he wanted to sing for the Lord, he was granted his wish, on the condition that he stay in Toccoa, the Georgia town where the Juvenile Training Institute was moved during Brown's three-year incarceration. Brown had met Bobby Byrd, an aspiring local singer and ballplayer, while still serving time, and Byrd's family gave him a temporary place to stay while he looked for permanent residence. Working as a janitor in a plastics factory and a helping hand at an Oldsmobile dealership, Brown soon joined several choirs with the help of Byrd's sister, Sarah. At first he resisted Byrd's efforts to get him to join his own group, the Avons, who had started out singing gospel before moving on to smooth vocal R&B. Brown's Ever Ready Gospel Singers, a spinoff of the larger Community Choir, cut an acetate of "His Eye Is on the Sparrow," and he was momentarily focused on getting airplay for it. But Byrd was persistent, and Brown soon agreed to join.

The Avons, renamed the Toccoa Band after learning of a preexisting group with the name, were an oversize vocal group—six original members before Brown—who accompanied themselves by stomping their feet. After a few weeks of rehearsals, Brown brought in Johnny Terry, who had just finished serving his own prison stint. As the group established itself on the local circuit, they took on a new name, the Flames, a play on the Torches, a popular biracial Toccoa-area band at the time. They also added rudimentary instrumentation, including a makeshift drum kit and electric guitar played by Nafloyd Scott, brother of original member Baby Roy Scott.

Brown, with his innate craving for the spotlight, began to steal it with his onstage maneuvers, borrowing from fads such as the camel walk, an old flapper-era step that had never quite gone out of vogue, and endlessly improvising other attention-grabbing contributions—dancing, for instance, with a dust mop at one high school appearance. Inspired by the group's steadily growing audience and a recent hit by the Orioles, "Baby, Please Don't Go," Brown wrote his second song, a heavily sanctified number in which he implored a lover to stay while his harmonizers burbled a lilting accompaniment. The Flames' yeoman vocal work was a sturdy hammock on which the aspiring frontman could sprawl in hammy agony. He called the song "Please Please Please."

Henry Stone was a Bronx-born Army veteran who landed in Los Angeles after World War II, where he began selling records for the four Bihari brothers, Saul, Jules, Lester, and Joe, who operated the independent blues and R&B label Modern Records and its affiliates. "There was no distribution in those days," says Stone. "I'd go to the railroad stations and sell stacks of 78s to the porters," who could get as much as three or four dollars apiece for records by Hadda Brooks and other rising stars in big cities starving for fresh music.

By the end of the decade Stone had moved to Miami, where he set out to be a big fish in what was then a very small pond. Having heard about a talented young singer and pianist from

the St. Augustine School for the Deaf and the Blind, he went
to see the young man, whose name was Ray Charles Robinson, perform in Miami. In the back of Stone's distribution warehouse, they recorded four songs in the singer's then-silky style,
unmistakably borrowed from Nat "King" Cole. It was one of the
first recording sessions for the singer now billing himself as Ray
Charles (to avoid confusion with the welterweight boxer Sugar
Ray Robinson).

By the mid-1950s Stone was firmly established with his De-
Luxe label, for which he had arranged a distribution deal with
Syd Nathan, proprietor of Cincinnati's King Records. The De-
Luxe imprint's breakout success came with a single released in
late 1954 by the vocal group the Charms. "Hearts of Stone" spent
nine weeks atop the R&B chart and quickly inspired a number-
one pop hit for the Fontane Sisters. It was the first million-seller
on King. With that feather in his cap, the Miami dealmaker was
entrusted with a good lead from Nathan, who had gotten wind
of a song that was the talk of central Georgia.

The Flames met Clint Brantley, a Macon nightclub owner
and talent scout, after making an impromptu appearance at
Bill's Rendezvous, a Toccoa nightclub where they'd become an
attraction. The headlining act that night was Little Richard,
who was so shaken by James Brown's audacious performance that
he apparently instructed his band director, Lucas "Fats" Gonder
(who would later tour with Brown), to introduce these upstarts
to Brantley, his manager. They auditioned over the weekend in
Brantley's office, singing the gospel standard "Looking for My
Mother" after the entrepreneur, suffering from a hangover, asked
for something sweet.

Suitably impressed, he helped the group relocate to Macon,

where the nightlife was thriving compared with Toccoa's. Brown, already married with two children and working as a janitor, was hungry for something more; with plenty of promises, he managed to get himself assigned a new parole officer in Macon. While the band continued to cultivate its audience, Brown's new affiliation with Brantley led to one of the more unusual experiences of his young life. Little Richard, just signed to Specialty Records in Los Angeles, was beginning to spend more time outside his home state, so his manager had the new protégé, Brown, fulfill several local commitments with Richard's band. As Richard's debut single, "Tutti-Frutti," began gathering momentum in the final weeks of 1955, the Flames—now being billed, on Brantley's suggestion, as the Famous Flames—needed a record of their own. They made arrangements to cut an acetate of "Please Please Please" in the studios of WIBB, a Macon radio station. The song in its demo form was an instant phenomenon on local radio, and Brantley began shopping for a label to give it a proper release.

"I got a call from Syd that in Macon there was a record breaking out," says Stone. "Says I should get in my car and check it out. At the same time, Ralph Bass, who was an A&R man for King and Federal, was in Birmingham. He was stationed in L.A., but he happened to be in Birmingham. Syd called him, too. He got there before I did." While Bass's head start on the highway earned him everlasting recognition as the man who "discovered" James Brown, Stone says he had a closer relationship with the singer in the early going. Like Bass, he predicted a smash hit for the record. He quickly brought the singer and his band to the Palms of Hallandale, a popular black nightspot in the Miami area, where they won over hundreds of new fans. When "Please

Please Please" was officially released the following spring, Stone helped promote it with radio stations throughout the South. He would remain a trusted confidant to Brown through the rest of the singer's life.

Despite the reservations of Nathan, who already had a reputation as a tough taskmaster with a tin ear for the rhythm and blues music he was selling, the Famous Flames were summoned to Cincinnati, where King housed its entire operation, from offices and recording studio to pressing plant and shipping warehouse, in a former Coca-Cola bottling plant on dead-end Brewster Avenue. On the fourth of February, 1956, James Brown and the Famous Flames entered the studio to record their official debut. Although Nathan reportedly stormed out of the control booth during the taping, Bass—an industry veteran who had delivered talent to the Black and White and Savoy labels before being recruited to head up Nathan's Federal imprint—managed to convince engineer Gene Redd to complete the session.

The son of a German-Jewish mother and an Italian-Catholic father, the late Bass grew up in the South Bronx, where, as he claimed in an interview in 1994, "I never saw a black until I was fourteen years old." Studying classical violin, he went to the Savoy Ballroom with a musician friend and was instantly smitten with rhythm and blues. As an A&R man, he helped establish careers for Hank Ballard, Texas guitarist T-Bone Walker, the Dominoes ("Sixty Minute Man"), and many others. "I was one of the few that started black music to go pop. I saw what was happening," Bass claimed. Supervising recording sessions, he was already known as a staunch advocate of spontaneity and raw emotion by the time he ushered in James Brown. "I didn't believe in no two-track [recording]," he recalled. "I believed in doing the thing, and that was it. I used to smoke a pack of ciga-rettes in three hours—you had to do four sides in three hours."

Ballard, in another 1994 interview, recalled the internal de-bate at King over the commercial potential of the "Please" sin-gle. Infamously, and by all accounts, Nathan deplored the song, complaining that it was repetitive and unmelodious. "Ralph Bass was a Russian [sic] Jew, but he had black ears!" whooped Ballard, a gregarious man who died in 2003. "Syd Nathan couldn't hear a hit if you put it in his lap. Ralph Bass was the salvation of the company. We knew it was a hit, but Syd Nathan hated it. He said, 'Nobody's gonna buy that shit! I thought the record was stuck!' "

But the record was not stuck. Based on cumulative regional successes built on the Flames' relentless touring schedule over the next several months, "Please Please Please" eventually climbed as high as number five on the R&B chart. Like the romantic-era pianist Franz Liszt, who thrilled audiences by col-lapsing in feigned hysterics at the overwhelming emotion of his own music, Brown brought down the house, night in and night out, with his melodramatic finale. The song would become the centerpiece of Brown's stage act for years to come, and it gave him still another nickname—Mr. Please Please Please. As the lyric strongly suggested, this young man—destitute and rootless as a child, undereducated and then confined as a teenager—was beginning to gain a national reputation as the man who would not be denied.

★ ★ ★ 5 ★ ★ ★

TRY ME

I f James Brown and Syd Nathan were in agreement on anything, it was their determination to capitalize on the surprise
success of "Please Please Please." From the spring of 1956,
when Brown's first hit lodged itself in the top ten of the national
R&B chart, through the summer of 1958, the singer released
nine more singles on King's Federal imprint. Some of them had
modest success regionally, primarily in the South. None of them
cracked the R&B top forty.

Nathan, a notorious penny-pincher, soon began to lose pa-
tience. After pressing for two years to repeat Brown's initial success, his attention was straying elsewhere. Hank Ballard and the
Midnighters, for instance, who had a strong run back in 1954
with a series of winking, good-natured songs for Federal beginning with "Work With Me Annie," were on the verge of a major
resurgence, as Ballard's "The Twist" began to show signs of set-

ting off a national dance craze. After busy years with Brown in 1956 and '57, Nathan refused to finance any recording sessions at all for the singer in 1958, preferring to release a solitary seven-inch record featuring "Begging, Begging," a remnant of a session from the previous October that was clearly a desperate attempt to revive the formula that had worked so well on "Please."

Brown's music at this point was still heavily indebted to the vocal-group rhythm and blues of the early 1950s, with occasional nods back to the jump blues of the previous decade ("I Feel That Old Feeling Coming On") or sideways toward the rambunctious New Orleans-style rock 'n' roll adopted by Brown's old acquaintance Little Richard ("Chonnie-On-Chon"). In what was quickly becoming a pattern between Brown and Nathan, the label boss declared no interest in the recording artist's new song, a romantic ballad in 6/8 time unaffected by any of Brown's already-familiar histrionics. In response, Brown reached into his own pocket for a recording session at King and had acetate copies pressed, which he offered to radio stations around Cincinnati, in Georgia, and in Nashville. A rush of advance orders finally convinced the cantankerous Nathan to invest in one more session, at Beltone Studios in New York, for the most persistent artist on his roster.

Like countless pop songs before and after, "Try Me" was a romantic ballad, an eyelash-batting overture to a love interest anchored by session player Ernie Hayes's solemn piano triplets, the sophisticated jazz guitar of Kenny Burrell (on a payday from his burgeoning career as a bop bandleader), and a creamy bridge played in tandem by the saxophonists George Dorsey and Clifford Scott. With the departure of Bobby Byrd, who would come and go many more times in the ensuing years, Brown was already onto his second set of Flames, with holdover Johnny Terry anchoring newcomers Bill Hollings, J.W. Archer, and Louis Madison. A classic school-gymnasium slow dance featuring the Flames' gentle gospel-style backing, "Try Me" was the product of a conscious effort to appeal to a crossover audience. "I knew I couldn't be too aggressive in front of mixed audiences," Brown would later explain. " 'Try Me' is written in the context of a man trying to romance a woman, yes, but it's also talking to the white people in the audience. You've tried all the others—how about trying me?" Though it remains one of the singer's best-known songs, it was arguably the only time in his career that Brown so evidently compromised the rawness that defined him in a play for commercial success.

The song climbed to number forty-eight on the Billboard pop chart, a telltale sign that there was an audience waiting for Brown across the country, not just in the inner cities and in the rural south. Despite the recognition, however, his live audiences would remain almost exclusively black for several years to come. Early bookings at the Apollo found him opening for Ballard and Little Willie John, fellow King Records artists who would come to have meaningful friendships with Brown. The Apollo, located in the heart of Harlem, quickly became one of Brown's most reliable venues. He and the band returned every few months for weeklong engagements, sometimes playing as many as seven shows a day. The Howard in Washington, D.C.; the Royal in Baltimore; the Regal in Chicago; the Uptown in Philadelphia; the Fox in Detroit—these were the best-known theaters along the unofficial tour route for African-American entertainers. But the so-called chitlin' circuit stretched as far south as Miami and west to Texas. "A few hip whites came, but not many," Brown recalled. "I remember one young man, a white kid, who slipped backstage at a gig in Florida in 1959 when I was still scuffling. He knew everything on the 'Please' album. I couldn't believe it."

He was experiencing a dilemma once described by Langston Hughes. "Blackness seen through black eyes may be too black for wide white consumption—unless coupled with greatness or its approximation," as the writer once explained. James Brown was an indefatigable performer. He was undoubtedly a showman, and his obvious feel for music, fueled by his gutty athleticism and his genuine love of the gospel tradition, came naturally to him. But his greatness was not yet fully apparent. "Try Me" may have been the sound of Brown polishing up his own act, but his talent was not for courtship. It was for coercion—the indoctrination of his audience by a fervor that might be considered spiritual, were it not so clearly earthbound. And the mainstream record-buying public, in a moment dominated almost as much by Perry Como, Ricky Nelson, and Johnny Mathis as by Elvis Presley, was not quite prepared to submit to that kind of relationship.

The most successful black pop stars of the 1950s were each compromised in some way. Chuck Berry, a savvy and somewhat cynical businessman who was already nearly thirty by the time of his first hit, ironed out his upbringing in the blues and enunciated his storytelling lyrics like a finishing-school instructor, ensuring maximum appeal to teenagers in chinos and loafers. Fats Domino, though arguably more influential than Presley, was marketed to the mainstream as a roly-poly teddy bear, genial and nonthreatening. New Orleans's Lloyd Price, who would become a close friend to Brown, belatedly capitalized on the breakthrough of his first R&B smash, "Lawdy Miss Clawdy," with a well-scrubbed version of the traditional folk tale "Stagger Lee," followed by the brassy nightclub tune "Personality." Brown's old Georgia associate, Little Richard, was easily the wildest of the bunch, but with his outrageous presence, his eyeliner, and his pursed lips, he was perceived less as a representative of any racial constituency than as an eccentric nonpareil.

Whatever their obvious talents, these men were each inescapably black in a country still woefully underprepared for integration. Even Nat King Cole, whose mellifluous, easygoing manner earned him a short-lived network variety program in 1956–57, was unable to sidestep the fact of his skin color. *The Nat King Cole Show*, a considerable ratings success, nevertheless succumbed to a lack of willing sponsors. In 1956 Cole was attacked onstage in Birmingham, Alabama. His reluctance to react with outrage over the incident—"Some of the worst bigots in the world own my records," he reasoned—earned him the dubious distinction of drawing the ire of future Supreme Court Justice Thurgood Marshall. Chief counsel for the NAACP at the time, Marshall suggested that Cole, if he was going to bow down to racism, should maybe switch to playing the banjo. Cole later made moves toward appeasement, taking out a lifetime membership in the Detroit chapter of the NAACP, consulting with President John F. Kennedy on race relations, and helping to organize the 1963 March on Washington. Yet he remained convinced that entertainment was not the place for politicking. "No one would want to listen to me," he said of the prospect of recording "message" songs like some of the underground folk singers of the time, "not even my fellow Negroes."

Following the careful example of the NAACP, most rights organizations were as yet unwilling to be seen as agitators. At the onset of the 1960s, Cole was just the sort of entertainer favored even by college-based groups such as the Student Nonviolent Coordinating Committee. High-profile performers such as Harry Belafonte and Sammy Davis, Jr., having proved themselves as marketable commodities to white audiences, were considered sensible spokesmen. As Booker T. Washington had suggested, black entertainers and athletes were bearing the burden of bringing blackness to attention in a nation monopolized by whites. But if the drive for civil rights depended largely on an expertly orchestrated media campaign of nonviolent resistance to irrational white anger, the rock 'n' roll crowd—of any color—was strapped with a reputation for violence.

Incidents at rock shows in and around Boston in the late 1950s were representative of similar experiences in major cities around the country. When a fifteen-year-old was stabbed and thrown onto the subway tracks after a concert, a police lieutenant told reporters that Negro youths were to blame and added, "We expect difficulty every time a rock 'n' roll show comes in." A Fats Domino appearance at an enlisted men's club at the naval station in Newport, Rhode Island, ended in a "bottle-throwing, chair-swinging riot," while Alan Freed's "Big Beat" caravan, featuring Berry and Jerry Lee Lewis, incited "packs of black-leather boys" to looting, stabbing, and robbing after an appearance at the Boston Arena. Boston Mayor John Hynes announced that his city would no longer rent public venues to promoters booking the new music, and his district attorney indicted Freed on an old anti-anarchy statute. "I am not against rock 'n' roll as such," Hynes said, but he was concerned about the "troublemakers" it seemed to attract.

Despite their growing mutual appreciation for the music,

black and white audiences would continue to be segregated in theaters across the South until well into the 1960s. Some promoters required one group to sit in the balcony while the other had the floor seats; in auditoriums, the color divide was often literalized with velvet rope bisecting the dance floor. But there was plenty of evidence that these mixed audiences, whether segregated or not, were helping to create a new generation of young people less inclined to judge a person based on the color of his or her skin. "The blacks on one side, whites on the other, digging how the blacks were dancing and copying them," recalled Ralph Bass. "Then, hell, the rope would come down, and they'd all be dancing together. And you know it was a revolution. . . . We did it as much with our music as the civil rights acts and all of the marches, for breaking the race thing down."

Columbia A&R executive Mitch Miller, the architect of a distinctly calculated brand of pop music that has often been ridiculed as antithetical to rock, actually recognized the social significance of the new youth music back in 1955, before it even had a commonly accepted name. "By their newfound attachment to rhythm and blues, young people might also be protesting the Southern tradition of not having anything to do with colored people," Miller wrote in the *New York Times Magazine*. "There is a steady—and healthy—breaking down of color barriers in the United States; perhaps the rhythm and blues rage—I am only theorizing—is another expression of it." *Cash Box*, then a leading music-industry trade magazine focused on jukebox sales, seconded the notion: "How better to understand what is known to you than by appreciation of the emotional experience of other people? And how better are the emotions portrayed than by music?"

In suburban Michigan in the 1950s, one young record collector was introduced to the music of Little Richard, Chuck Berry, Bo Diddley, and other new artists on Nashville's WLAC—"50,000 watts of clear channel power." WLAC was operated by "white men who were totally out of their wigs for black music," recalls John Sinclair, though at first the young man was unclear about the identities of the musicians. Digging for information about these rowdy songwriters who were setting his world on fire, he quickly decided he had an affinity for these men struggling to make a place for themselves in a hostile world. A decade later, acting as manager for the politically motivated Detroit rock band MC5, he would cofound the White Panther Party.

Wayne Cochran, the white soul singer who befriended and sometimes performed with James Brown, was often mistaken as a black performer from recordings such as his remake of Bob & Earl's "Harlem Shuffle." He remembers taking Otis Redding to a Dairy Queen for an ice cream cone, where his friend was told that Negroes were required to go around back for service. "I said, 'This is ridiculous. Sell it to me,' and I handed it to him," says Cochran. Having grown up in an all-white neighborhood in small-town Georgia, Cochran believes that soul music "did as much to integrate this country as the marches did. It got to where we didn't see a separation."

"In many ways," James Brown himself would claim, "the entire civil rights movement began when a white kid in the audience stood up and cheered for a black performer." In the North, Brown continued to draw predominantly black crowds, given that the theaters he played were mostly located in the inner cities. But in the South, where even the fiercest segregationists were often more accustomed to coexistence with black neighbors than liberal white Northerners, Brown's audiences were becoming more mixed as he began to settle onto the pop charts—"Think" in 1960, "Bewildered" in 1961, and, the following year, "Night Train," a spunky cover of a well-traveled R&B instrumental with roots in music by members of Duke Ellington's band. On that song, Brown called out a conductor's itinerary of whistle stops: "Miami, Florida! Atlanta, Georgia! Raleigh, North Carolina! Washington, D.C. Oh, and Richmond, Virginia, too. Baltimore, Philadelphia. New York City. Take me home! Boston, Massachusetts." As the critic Dave Marsh once wrote, by adding this hollered litany the singer turned a once-wordless tune "into the saga of the black man in America, his travels from South to North."[1]

In late September 1963, as the country was convulsing over the Birmingham church bombing that left four schoolgirls dead, Brown and his revue appeared at one of his usual stops, the Municipal Auditorium in New Orleans. In the venerable *Louisiana*

---

[1] "Night Train," in a much slower, more methodical 1952 version by tenor saxophonist and onetime Ellington sideman Jimmy Forrest, was well-known as the training music of choice for the menacing heavyweight champion Sonny Liston, who took the crown from Floyd Patterson in 1962. To many, the lumbering, expressionless young man from Sand Slough, Arkansas, represented the impending uprising of black America. Having been imprisoned as a teenager and employed by the St. Louis mafia as a debt collector, Liston was made a pariah in the national press, disowned by the NAACP and called "King of the Beasts" by *Look* magazine. Brown, whose own youthful branding as a good-for-nothing was not so distant in his memory, was one of the few celebrities to come to Liston's defense. He wasn't the worst person in the world, Brown said, in what amounted to one of his earliest patent declarations of black pride. Sonny Liston "should not be treated like he's the world's first public figure to have a record of being in trouble," he told a reporter.

Weekly, the voice of the state's black constituency since the first years of the century, columnist Elgin Hychew celebrated the peaceful mingling of black and white at the show. "Our hearts really throbbed at seeing the people of this community enjoying themselves without incident," he wrote. "We saw white girls and Negro girls, white boys and Negro boys seated side by side and together whooping it up."

Around this time Brown moved north, to the elite black neighborhood of St. Albans, Queens, where his neighbors at one time or another included Du Bois, Jackie Robinson, Joe Louis, Count Basie, and John Coltrane. He purchased the house from trumpeter Cootie Williams of the Ellington band, painting the distinctive twelve-room Victorian black. In 1964 he scheduled a homecoming concert for himself at Augusta's Bell Auditorium. On an earlier return to his hometown, he had headlined a show at the local ballpark, Jennings Stadium, where the mixed crowd paid no mind to the segregated seating arrangement and "integrated themselves," in Brown's words. But the Bell Auditorium show took place with Brown's white fans sequestered together in the section behind the stage. Never again, he vowed afterward: "I had grown up with the signs that said WHITE DRINKING WATER and COLORED DRINKING WATER, and it always seemed to me that water didn't have any color." Brown refused to play his next engagement, in Macon, until city officials agreed not to enforce Jim Crow policy.

Brown's lifelong insistence on professional appearance and demeanor among his musicians—into his last years, he still forbade members from wearing jeans on airline flights—was a direct result of his efforts to ensure hotel rooms and restaurant service for the band in the days of Jim Crow. Saxophonist Pee

Wee Ellis, who joined the band in 1965, has clear memories of lingering antipathies in the South. Ellis grew up in Rochester, New York, after the racially motivated murder of his stepfather in Lubbock, Texas, in 1955. In the summer of 1957, while visiting an aunt in New York City, he spotted Sonny Rollins on the street and impetuously asked the saxophonist whether he gave lessons. For months, the teenaged Ellis flew from Rochester to the big city and back every Wednesday to study with the budding jazz colossus. The plane tickets, he says, were twenty-five dollars. Still in high school, Ellis gigged six nights a week around Rochester with other young jazz and R&B players, including the bassist Ron Carter and trumpeter Waymon Reed. Reed, who died in 1983, was the man who brought Ellis into Brown's band; he was married for years to the singer Sarah Vaughan.

In 1960, Ellis went to Miami to visit a cousin, and he decided to stay. There, he started a band called Dynamics, Inc. When the Beatles broke through in America, Ellis's group worked a set of the British act's songs into its repertoire. "With Beatle wigs," he says. "Five black guys." The group landed plenty of work around Miami's dance clubs, such as the Peppermint Lounge. The nightclubs were strictly whites-only, and the band was treated like the hired help. "In fact," Ellis says, "we were not privileged to access the front door. You had to have a police card, and after work you got out of Dodge. We had to eat in the kitchen—that kind of bullshit."

Ellis's wife, Barbara, joined the band on the road during the time of the Watts riots. Having met the saxophonist in Miami, where they were arrested three times for consorting, she was nevertheless unprepared for the indignity that awaited them on a tour stop in Charlotte, North Carolina. Local police officers broke into their room in the middle of the night and asked for their marriage license. Though they had a child together by this time, the couple was not officially married, and they were arrested. Trombonist Levi Raspbury stayed behind while the band went on to its next gig, arranging for the Ellises' release with the help of civil liberties lawyers. (Eventually, says Barbara Ellis, they beat the case, setting a precedent that forced North Carolina to acknowledge common-law marriage.)

In the early 1960s, injustice was not yet an explicit subject of black singers' lyrical repertoires, as it would become later in the decade. The looming issue of civil rights was, however, already well established as a theme in the less commercially circumscribed realms of folk and jazz music. Acoustic artists such as Odetta and Big Bill Broonzy sang of the plight of black Americans—both by way of metaphor and, as on Broonzy's "Black, Brown and White," in frank, unmistakable terms. Bob Dylan, Phil Ochs, and Tom Paxton were among the most prominent of the many Greenwich Village–bred folk singers who made a habit of writing songs based on headlines from the morning newspapers, denouncing in particular the state of Mississippi for its opposition to integration and its setting for the murders of the activists Medgar Evers and Chaney, Goodman, and Schwerner. Most notably, "We Shall Overcome," the folk hymn adapted by Pete Seeger from an old gospel standard, was fast becoming the theme song of the movement.

From the era of bop, many jazz musicians were more interested in intellectualism and artistry than the marketplace, a reordering of priorities that resulted in a small but weighty catalog of socially conscious recordings. As Langston Hughes once put it, the bebop revolution was itself a kind of statement. "You must not know where Bop comes from," says Jesse B. Semple, Hughes's long-running fictional mouthpiece. "From the police beating Negroes' heads . . . Every time a cop hits a Negro with his billy club, that old club say, 'BOP! BOP! . . . BE-BOP! . . . MOP! . . . BOP!' " Recordings such as Rollins's *Freedom Suite*, Ornette Coleman's *Free Jazz*, and Charles Mingus's "Haitian Fight Song" (which, said the composer, "could just as well be called 'Afro-American Fight Song' ") helped mark a period of musical challenges that were equally intended as social recriminations. The singer Abbey Lincoln shrugged off plans to mold her career as a Julie London–style lounge starlet in favor of a cultural awareness inspired in part by her relationship with the drummer Max Roach, with whom she recorded the searing free-jazz song cycle *We Insist! Max Roach's Freedom Now Suite* (1960). Her 1957 tune "Strong Man," written by Oscar Brown, Jr., was an early indication that she would actively engage her audience in a dialogue about its image of black America. "Hair crisp and curly and cropped kinda close / Picture a lover like this," she sang admiringly, at a time when many African-Americans still wore their hair in the processed style that was a James Brown trademark.

The world of rhythm and blues, more committed to record sales than folk and jazz, was a bit more reluctant, at least initially, to take up the appeal for equal rights. With the mainstream success of soul stars such as Ray Charles and Sam Cooke and the rapid rise of Berry Gordy's Motown label (touting itself as "The Sound of Young America"), fellow R&B acts were concerned about jeopardizing their own crossover potential by taking a political stance. This was a time, after all, when black Americans pushing for social justice were routinely referred to as "uppity."

A few veteran pop stars, such as Belafonte and Davis, gladly lent their celebrity on behalf of rallies and protest marches; like Nat King Cole, they were among the key organizers of the landmark March on Washington in the summer of 1963. But less financially secure entertainers, scrambling for bookings in homely auditoriums thousands of miles from Las Vegas, sometimes assumed that sort of commitment to be a short path toward career endangerment. Black performers who depended in large part on Southern audiences often couldn't afford to make their personal views public. Historically, there had been only occasional, isolated incidents of pop songs that asked listeners to confront the shame of institutionalized racism. "Strange Fruit," the bleak ballad of Southern lynching immortalized by Billie Holiday, was surely the most famous, and most apparent. In jukeboxes and on radio playlists, "brown" was sometimes submitted as a softer alternative to black, as in Nellie Lutcher's 1948 hit "Fine Brown Frame," or Oscar Brown, Jr.'s "Brown Baby," recorded by Mahalia Jackson and Nina Simone.

Belafonte, whose movement credentials were impeccable, would later express dismay at the lack of cooperation he'd been able to enlist from many of the best-known black entertainers of the period: "Especially in black America, where I thought my task would be easier, I found enormous resistance. When the time came for show and tell, nobody showed, they had nothing to tell." Cooke, the Motown artists, Brown—"all of these people distanced themselves from the movement; not only once removed from it, but sometimes twenty times removed from it, I think."

It was Cooke, however, who would decisively push soul music into the midst of the civil rights struggle. The onetime gospel singer's heavyhearted anthem, "A Change Is Gonna Come," inspired by Dylan's "Blowin' in the Wind," was released posthumously in early 1965, two months after the singer's murder in Los Angeles.

The other figure to envision soul music as an ideal medium between the guarded hopes of black America and the growing enlightenment of the white majority was Chicagoan Curtis Mayfield. Assuming leadership of the vocal group the Impressions following the early departure of Jerry Butler, the beatific Mayfield took the group into the pop top ten in the wake of the Birmingham church bombing with the restorative "It's All Right." That release was followed in June 1964 by another top-ten hit, "Keep on Pushing." Whereas the first song was unspecific in its intentions beyond a quiet urge toward peace and calm, the second was less ambiguous. Here Mayfield established his great theme—upward mobility. Whether the goal may be heavenly acceptance, worldly accomplishment, or the elemental aim of self-respect, the direction is always skyward, and the Impressions under Mayfield were patently invested in the business of keeping heads held high. After yet another top-ten showing with a sweet-natured version of "Amen," the group ushered in the year 1965 with their most hopeful testament to date, "People Get Ready," a biblical reassurance that the promised land was near.

Brown, meanwhile, was headed in another direction, though his too had a distinct upward trajectory. To the astonishment of Syd Nathan, *Live at the Apollo* became the second-best-selling album in the country, remaining on the pop album chart for sixty-six weeks. The album confirmed what initiates already knew—that Brown's live show, with its maniacal energy and its perfectly calibrated mood swings, far surpassed anything he had yet managed to achieve in the recording studio. For nearly a decade he had been knocking around with well-tested formulas—the hat-in-hand serenade of "Try Me," the Ellingtonian bustle of "Night Train," a snazzy (if unnecessary) orchestral remake of Louis Jordan's "Caldonia." He had a clandestine hit in 1960 with "(Do the) Mashed Potatoes (Pt. 1)," a shuffling novelty song cut for Henry Stone's Dade label to spite Syd Nathan. After the failure of an instrumental single credited to Brown's then-bandleader, James (J. C.) Davis, Nathan had declined to finance Brown's interest in further sessions geared toward the red-hot market for economical, saxophone-driven dance fads. Though an instrumental, the original track featured Brown hollering variations on the phrase "mashed potatoes," the name of a popular heel-swiveling dance step—"Hash brown potatoes! . . . French fried potatoes!" Later, Stone overdubbed Brown's voice with that of the similarly raspy Miami disc jockey Carlton "King" Coleman. The song was credited to Nat Kendrick and the Swans, after Brown's drummer at the time. Its surprise success—top-ten R&B—convinced Nathan to let Brown start cutting instrumentals at King.

Three years later Brown had his biggest pop hit yet with a melodramatic, string-showered version of the pop standard "Prisoner of Love," which had been a major chart record for Como, Billy Eckstine, and, way back in 1932, for Russ Columbo. The song, arranged by Sammy Lowe—best known for his work with Sammy Davis, the Platters, and Sam Cooke, among others—had special connotation for Brown, who clearly identified more with the actuality of imprisonment than the metaphoric shackles of unrequited love. In the pictorial words of Dave Marsh, Brown sounds on this single like "a man trying to fight his way out of a fog."

Despite the unprecedented success of the live album, the fog didn't really begin to lift for Brown until mid-1964. The band, as ever, was in transition. This time, however, the changes were wholesale. New member Nat Jones, who played saxophone and organ, became the musical director, and Melvin and Maceo Parker, young brothers from the small city of Kinston, North Carolina, signed on as drummer and saxophonist, respectively. This core group, with veteran holdovers St. Clair Pinckney on tenor, Les Buie on guitar, and Bernard Odum on bass, came together to create the beginnings of a radical new sound. On the short (barely over two minutes) but instantly mood-setting song that marked the first session for the newly revamped band, the saxophones answer Brown's pickup lines like the sly chatter of yes men. It's as though the singer were making a move on a comely new lady friend on a street corner, egged on by a small clique of sidekicks murmuring their amused approval from a darkened doorway behind him.

The fact that Brown called the song "Out of Sight" was in itself significant: it indicated a sense that his own personal hipness could be commodified. The phrase, which originated in the Bowery slang of the late 1800s (it appears in the work of the literary realist Stephen Crane), had been for years part of the jazz vernacular. "What we need," Brown would say in a few years, when his activism on behalf of the poor grew from giving away turkeys on Thanksgiving to advocating social reform on national news and talk shows, "are programs that are so out of sight they'll leave the militants with their mouths open."

Tellingly, "Out of Sight" was recorded mere weeks before a less innovative yet aptly titled tune, "Maybe the Last Time," which spelled the end of the Famous Flames, the backup singers whose churchy accompaniment had kept Brown's music firmly planted in the golden age of doo-wop. More than ever, Brown was prepared to rely on the progressive instincts of his rhythm section and the hard bop interplay of his growing stable of jazz-trained horn players. "When people talk about soul music they talk only about gospel and R&B coming together," as he noted in his autobiography. "That's accurate about a lot of soul, but if you're going to talk about mine, you have to remember the jazz in it." With its brassy bursts of punctuation, like the multiple exclamation points of an action comic book, "Out of Sight" bears much more than a passing resemblance to "Papa's Got a Brand New Bag," the song which, paired with "I Got You (I Feel Good)," is generally credited as the one-two punch of Brown's true arrival as a pop revolutionary.

But the shift away from 1950s rock 'n' roll toward something more uniquely his own was slower in coming than Brown might have liked. For a time his career was tied up in legal wrangling, as the singer and Ben Bart attempted to distance themselves from the intractable Mr. Nathan. In 1963 they set up Brown's own production company, Fair Deal, attempting to exploit a loophole in King's archaic contract language with Brown (the singer was signed as a solo vocalist, for "personal services"). Entertainment lawyer Marty Machat brokered an association between Fair Deal and Smash, a division of Mercury Records, to release new music under the James Brown banner. When Smash released "Out of Sight" and "Maybe the Last Time" on a two-sided single in July 1964, Nathan sued.

By court order, Smash was forbidden to release future music containing Brown's vocals. Over the next three years, however, Smash would release several albums credited to Brown, instrumental grab bags with the singer sometimes featured on organ and the band covering contemporary hits such as Wilson Pickett's "634-5789 (Soulsville, U.S.A.)" and Dyke and the Blazers' "Funky Broadway." King and Brown eventually reconciled, with the singer demanding, and receiving, a far more favorable royalty structure. Under the tutelage of a Bay Area producer, record-shop owner, and impresario named Ray Dobard, Brown had been studying the ways that recording acts were historically disadvantaged by their contracts. In his new deal with King, he would claim to be the first recording artist, other than classical composers, to command a 10 percent royalty rate.

The next piece of the puzzle to fall into place was guitarist Jimmy Nolen, recruited from Johnny Otis's band in California by tenor saxophonist Eldee Williams. Nolen, an Oklahoma native who had developed a bluesy style that owed a debt to the Texan T-Bone Walker, recorded a handful of essentially unnoticed singles for King's Federal label in the 1950s before joining Otis's popular band. With an onomatopoetic nickname, "Chank," that described the rhythmic habit he had of playing slashing, lightly muted chords on hollow-body guitars, Nolen picked up where Brown's previous guitarist, Les Buie, left off, adding another layer of percussive effect to the ensemble sound. "I was hearing everything, even the guitars, like they were drums," explained Brown in an often-quoted passage from his autobiography. "Later on they said it was the beginning of funk. I just thought of it as where my music was going."

★ ★ ★ 6 ★ ★ ★

COLD SWEAT

He'd heard the rumbling. Some activists in Boston were demanding to know why this proud black man, this hero to African-Americans across the country, would be working with the government to placate their city in a moment so charged with justifiable outrage. Bryant Rollins, then of the New Urban League of Greater Boston, was a former *Boston Globe* reporter and a founder of the *Bay State Banner*, the city's African-American newspaper. With other community leaders, he had called for Brown to come into Roxbury to speak with residents. When that didn't happen, they boycotted the show. To Rollins and others, Brown's call for civility was utterly misguided.

Onstage, Brown took pains to make clear his intentions were good, and that he was not doing the government's bidding. "My fight," he said, "is to make the black man see that he can be first-class and think first-class. . . . I want you to know that I have been paid to say nothing. I mean, I'm my own man. I own myself. Nobody own[s] me. I can say what I want to say."

Brown knew the balance was delicate between sounding genuinely concerned and merely high and mighty. "Last night I was in Harlem, during all the problems, in the midst of it," he told the crowd. "Because I don't want to be a cat sittin' up high, lookin' down and sayin', 'What are they doin'?'—I was down there. I might live in society but my heart's in the ghetto, 'cause that's where I was born, you see? And as long as the black man got a problem, I got it."

The immediate problem, as he saw it, was that young black men were putting themselves in harm's way by rioting. To Brown, that kind of reaction was little more than a "suicide mission," an invitation for retaliation by law enforcement. As he later told the Rev. Al Sharpton, a close associate, "I saw people setting themselves up to kill themselves. Here was a trap. We killed King. We'll kill everybody if there's riots. I wanted to stop people from killing themselves." Like Marcus Garvey, who once wrote a song called "Keep Cool" for his irate supporters when he was hauled off to the Atlanta Federal Penitentiary on charges of mail fraud, Brown resorted to music.

That weekend, Brown was by no means the only prominent figure calling for restraint. In Washington, D.C., Stokely Carmichael strode through the chaotic streets shouting "Not now!" and telling agitators to "stay off the streets if you don't have a gun." In Oakland, members of the Black Panthers did much the same.

More moderate voices, too, worried that overwrought emotions would lead to further bloodshed. Jackie Robinson ex-essed his concern about "repercussions." Adam Clayton

Powell, the deposed congressman, lamented, "It was going to be a long, hot summer anyway. . . . Disillusioned young people in the King camp are going to ally themselves with the black militants." CORE's Floyd McKissick believed reactionary violence was now inescapable. "The philosophy of nonviolence died with Dr. King, the last prince of nonviolence," he said bitterly. "Black Americans will no longer tolerate this killing of their males. No other man in the country is capable of carrying on the philosophy of nonviolence."

But James Brown was not resigned to the inevitability of further violence. In crisis, he was ready to flex his own considerable power of persuasion. Not that he was a proponent of King's viewpoint, exactly; he'd always been hesitant to commit to complete nonviolence. To the singer, doctrine in any form was just another form of enslavement. "I must create a system or be enslaved by another man's," as William Blake declared. As much as his irresistible music, Brown's absolute insistence on self-reliance made him a modern-day folk hero. It was also what made him a one-of-a-kind figure as the civil rights era tumbled toward its conclusion. Brown, recalls Sharpton, was steadfast in traveling his own road. At a time when black Americans felt compelled to choose sides between the philosophies of Dr. King and Stokely Carmichael, James Brown followed no man.

At the Garden, the time had come for Brown to acknowledge the assassination. Typically, it was not in his constitution to let any hardship, no matter how cruel, impede the forward progress of the show. Five years later, he would greet the devastating news of the death of his oldest son, Teddy, in a car crash, by setting his jaw and forging ahead with three straight engagements : Columbus, Dayton, and Buffalo.

"We got to pay our respects to the late, great, incomparable—somebody we love very much, and I have all the admiration in the world for—I got a chance to know him personally—the late, great, Mr. Martin Luther King," Brown fumbled, breaking the ice by speaking King's name. After praising Atkins ("This man has been able to call the shots ever since I been here") and promising all the hit songs his fans had come to expect (" 'Can't Stand Myself,' 'Please,' 'Try Me' "), he urged those present at the Garden to hurry home after the show to watch it again, when it would be rebroadcast. "Look, I want you to go to school and get yourself together so tomorrow, you have a better chance than we've had," he said. "When the show is over, go home and catch the show again. So holler loud when you hear something you like, because you can see it on TV again tonight as you go back home.

"Get it off your chest right now," James Brown urged.

He had Kevin White waiting in the wings, but first Brown introduced Atkins, the city councilor. "Makes me feel good to see a black man in the driver's seat," Brown told the audience. Atkins was a fast-emerging political figure in Boston, part of a new breed of elected officials representing the growing impact of black and progressive voters across the nation. In November, Cleveland's Carl Stokes had been elected the first black mayor of a major American city. Also in 1967, Walter Washington had been appointed Mayor-Commissioner of the District of Columbia by President Johnson. Their inaugurations followed by a year the ascendance of Percy Sutton, a New York City lawyer perhaps best known for representing Malcolm X, to the position of Manhattan Borough President, a seat that he won in a landslide. (A force in Manhattan politics for years to come, Sutton would be instrumental in the revival of the Apollo Theater in the 1980s.)

The year 1966 also saw Massachusetts voters make the state's attorney general, Republican Ed Brooke, the first popularly elected African-American senator. Before becoming attorney general, Brooke had lost a bid to become secretary of state to a young Kevin White. During that campaign, supporters of his opponent had distributed bumper stickers that read VOTE WHITE. When Brooke complained about the implication, White turned the tables, accusing Brooke of being the guilty party in terms of racial insinuation.

Brooke, elected to the Senate the same year that Carmichael debuted his call for Black Power, was a prominent example of the kind of political assimilation that was increasingly being treated with disdain by the radical elements of the civil rights struggle. He was, for one thing, an unapologetic Republican, loyal to the party of Lincoln, the great emancipator, son of a Veteran's Administration lawyer who had once questioned Marcus Garvey's "back to Africa" crusade by asking, "Why would I go back when I have never been there?" The younger Brooke was suspicious of the traditional Democratic Party machinery, especially in a state dominated by vote-grafting, office-hopping leaders such as the late James Michael Curley, the perennially incumbent mayor of Boston and onetime governor of Massachusetts who "once ran successfully for reelection to Congress from his jail cell," as Brooke noted in his autobiography. A key contributor to the Kerner Commission's 1967 study on civil disturbance, Brooke was proudly centrist, a position that did not ingratiate him to black leaders less interested in securing the common ground. He once met with H. Rap Brown, the SNCC chairman a incoming justice minister for the Black Panthers, "in a shabby basement apartment on Seventh Avenue in Harlem." According to Brooke, the man famous for claiming that "violence is necessary, as American as cherry pie" told the senator that he was part of the white establishment. "You're not black," Brown reportedly told Brooke. "You're not one of us. . . . You are what's wrong with America."

But Brooke shot back: "What's wrong with being in the U.S. Senate?" he asked. "That's where the power is."

Tom Atkins surely would have agreed. Speaking with the late filmmaker Henry Hampton, producer of the monumental PBS series *Eyes on the Prize*, the former councilor discussed how he'd always been convinced that the way to fight injustice was to make the system work on your behalf. "You're gonna have to be extra vigilant, sometimes a little boisterous, willing to be obnoxious," he said, but the place to do that was inside the system. "Survival becomes a more compelling argument than destruction," he said. "I bet on survival."

Atkins understood power, and he saw it in James Brown. He was, in fact, a bit starstruck. "He told me I could sit in his seat, but I know I can't fill his shoes," the bespectacled legislator told the Garden crowd as he stepped to the microphone. "He's the greatest." Atkins recognized Brown's spreading cultural influence, mentioning the singer's just-concluded visit to the Ivory Coast and his upcoming commitment to entertain military troops in Vietnam. "This country owes a great thing to James Brown," he said, "and we're lucky that we have him here tonight with us."

Then the councilor began introducing Kevin White, who was nding off to the side with several uniformed members of the

Boston police force, still trying to remember the singer's name. "He called him James Washington a couple of times," says Dick Flavin, then the mayor's press secretary.

Atkins bit his tongue about the afternoon's tense negotiations. "The man whose foresight and leadership have given the city of Boston and the whole metropolitan area a new lease on life," he offered graciously. "He's a man who's young, he's a man who cares, and he's gonna make this a great city," he continued, to faint applause.

Brown, sensing an uncomfortable reception for the mayor, cut in front of the councilor. He'd had the pleasure of meeting the mayor before the show, the singer said. "This," he said, "is a swingin' cat."

Many years after the show, White reconstructed the moment in an interview on WGBH. "The Gahdens is dahk," he recalled, with his unreformed Boston accent and locals-only habit of pluralizing the name of the arena. As he stepped under the harsh spotlight, "for a moment I thought, you know, someone could take a pop at me from the balcony. Someone could take a shot at me."

The mayor's entourage and Brown's band were similarly anxious about the crowd. Marva Whitney, who was the singer's companion at the time, reasoned that if Brown's capacity for spellbinding was enough to subdue a riot, there were those who might believe he could also incite one. They'd said much the same about Malcolm X a decade before, when he'd calmed an incensed mob of two thousand outside a Harlem police precinct, where a member of the Nation of Islam had been hauled during a violent confrontation with officers. It was, remarked one police official ominously, "too much power for one man to have

Into the glare at the Garden stepped the mayor, who knew, in spite of the intimidation, that he was being granted a unique opportunity to try on the role of peacemaker, in front of the television cameras, thanks to the popularity of this street-talking soul singer. "All of us are here tonight to listen to a great talent— James Brown," White began tentatively, rumbling his words from the back of his throat, as if to clear away his nerves. He and Brown shared faint, fleeting smiles, in mutual agreement that the mayor was no authority on the singer's talent. "But we're also here to pay tribute to one of the greatest Americans, Dr. Martin Luther King.

"Twenty-four hours ago, Dr. King died, for all of us—black and white," the mayor bellowed, his voice rising, his face ashen, making a fist and jabbing a finger in the murky direction of the unseen seats. "That we may live together in harmony, without violence and in peace." His pace was methodical, deliberate; he couldn't afford to be misunderstood.

"Now I'm here tonight, like all of you, to listen to James. But I'm also here to ask for your help. I'm here to ask you to stay with me as your mayor, and to make Dr. King's dreams a reality in Boston." The response, while tepid, was respectful; there was a sense that, with each pause for punctuation, the mayor was winning over a skeptical audience. "This is our city, and its future is in our hands, tonight, tomorrow, and the days that follow.

"Martin Luther King loved this city, and it's up to our generation to prove his faith in us. So all I ask you tonight is this: Let us look at each other, here in the Gardens and back at home, and pledge that no matter what any other community might do, we in Boston will honor Dr. King in peace. Thank you."

It was an arresting moment. In delivering his half-desperate call for unity, the mayor had summoned some of the thundering accentuations of Dr. King himself.

Years later, White credited Brown for cushioning his reception by calling him a "swingin' cat." "You'd think we were born in the same nursery when he got through," said the former mayor. "He was effusive. My mother hadn't spoken that well of me during the campaign. And of course, he put me immediately at ease, and he married me to the audience, which I could not have done myself in that environment."

Even in the most somber of situations, life to Brown was a groove. As the mayor strode offstage to applause and some cheering, the singer said a few words in praise—"He's a young man, so he's thinking together. . . . The man is together!" He asked for another round of applause for the mayor, and got it. Then he jumped back into the business at hand. As he began warbling about doing the Boogaloo and the Funky Broadway, one of the musicians (probably Ellis) laid down a sustained chord on the organ, like the anticipatory pause in a Baptist church service. "Unh," Brown grunted, seconding himself: "Unh! . . . Good God." Suddenly, the band lurched into action, and the singer pitched himself into the opening refrain of "That's Life."

Recently written for Frank Sinatra, "That's Life" had given the singer a rare appearance on the R&B chart in 1966. With its tale of hard knocks and the fortitude to overcome them ("Each time I find myself flat on my face / I pick myself up and get back in the race"), "That's Life" struck a chord with soul singers in the season of the Meredith March, the murder of Malcolm X, and the infamous Moynihan report on the shortcomings of "The Negro Family." Brown's performance of the song at his second *Live at the Apollo* taping in June 1967 coincided with studio re cordings by Aretha Franklin, the Temptations, and Los Angeles's O. C. Smith.

Never before, however, had Brown's mutating version of the song—sometimes ponderous and string-laden, sometimes, as at the Garden, galloping and breathless—sounded so uncanny. If the verse about "ridin' high in April / shot down in May" was not quite timed to describe the present crisis, it seemed all the more eerie as Brown hurtled through the line, "Some people get their kicks from stomping on a dream." The singer had been a puppet, a pauper, a pirate, a poet, a pawn, and a king. Now he was being asked to take on the role of a white knight.

In the Sinatra original, the singer may be blithe, but he's not unaffected. If things don't pick up by July, he says in the last line, he'll just "roll myself up in a big ball, and die." For Brown, however, delivering those words was inconceivable. He'll roll himself up in a big ball, all right. Then, as he hollered at the Garden, he'll get a soul sister from over here, and a soul sister from over there. The song typically ended with the band answering his call for witnesses with a series of "yeah"s, followed by a brassy flourish and a wordless Brown holler. In Boston, he effectively beat the song down, as if to throttle any notion of despair. "Got to have a GOOD time!" he wailed. "Whoa, yeah! Whoa, yeah! Hey. Hey! *Yeeeeeooooow!*"

He had known it his whole life: It felt good to scream. "I feel like I want to scream," as he announced countless times in concert. "Is it all right if I scream? Can I get down and scream one time?" As a youth in Augusta, he was taught to lift his voice in church. The desire to be heard, of course, has a long tradition in religious worship. The roots of "shout" music—of the sort prac-ticed in Bishop Daddy Grace's House of Prayer, for instance—

can be traced to the book of Joshua: "And it came to pass at the seventh time, when the priests blew with the trumpets, Joshua said unto the people, Shout, for the Lord hath given you the city." Frederick Law Olmsted, observing a black church service in New Orleans in the mid-nineteenth century, was struck by the "shouts, and groans, terrific shrieks, and indescribable expressions of ecstasy—of pleasure and agony."

For Brown, the instinct came naturally. "I know hardship," as he once told *Jet* magazine. "I was born shaking hands with it."

"I know what it means," as Brown would testify on 1973's twelve-minute soul-search "Mind Power," "being nine years old before I got my first pair of underwear out of a store." But admissions like those were comparatively rare, old memories best left boxed up in the attic. That's what James Brown did with his memories. When his estranged mother once showed up at his door backstage at the Apollo, he coldly kept her waiting. Yet if he systematically denied his own pain, by 1968 he was braced to accept the broader burden of black America's torment.

★ ★ ★ **7** ★ ★ ★

SOUL PRIDE, PT. 1

"To get people to listen to you, you first have to get their attention," James Brown told *Time* magazine in 1966. It was a bit of self-evident advice that he had been pursuing with all of his being for years. If anyone was going to qualify as a superstar, it was going to be James Brown. Under the guidance of Ben Bart, founder of the Universal Attractions booking agency, to whom the singer had come on an enthusiastic recommendation from Hank Ballard, Brown pushed hard for recognition beyond his core audience through the middle years of the 1960s, seeking—and finding—white fans.

In Brown, Ben Bart recognized a man who would go after fame and fortune the way a wolverine goes after a field mouse. The older man would tell the singer, "You're going to be the biggest artist in show business someday," something even Brown sometimes doubted. But he certainly had the energy to try. The

elder Bart, a paternal figure who felt comfortable calling the otherwise relentlessly formal singer "Jimmy" (Brown, in turn, called
him "Pop"), went on the road with Brown for several years, securing enough live dates—more than three hundred a year—to
earn the singer the title "The Hardest Working Man in Show
Business." Together they built their audience by making each
appearance a complete spectacle, like Bishop Daddy Grace or
Silas Green from New Orleans.

In the early years, Brown shared stages with chitlin' circuit
comedy legends such as Dewey "Pigmeat" Markham and Jackie
"Moms" Mabley, both of whom had careers that stretched back
to the 1920s, and nearly every R&B and soul act of note. Bart
taught Brown the efficiency of developing a self-contained
bill, and the James Brown show came to include female dancers called the Brownies (later, the Brownettes, then the Jewels,
and in the last years of his life, the Bittersweets); comedy from
Clay Tyson (brother of the actress Cicely Tyson) or saxophonist
Maceo Parker; and a stable of opening acts, usually the Revue's
own featured singers and other Brown subordinates with new
singles to promote.

Together, Ben Bart and James Brown attracted fast-growing
audiences in part by raffling off prizes such as fur coats and cars,
thousands of dollars worth of merchandise a night. At the 1962
shows recorded for *Live at the Apollo,* crowds lined around the
block were shivering in the autumn air. The elder Bart suggested
the musicians serve the fans coffee. And so they did. Giving
some to get some was a key part of Brown's business philosophy,
to a fault. Local disc jockeys were often invited to introduce
Brown onstage, then quietly handed envelopes filled with large
bills. (Winking practices like that eventually drew the performer

some unwanted attention: in the early 1970s, Brown's right-hand man, Charles Bobbit, would be subpoenaed in a payola investigation centered on the star New York disc jockey Frankie Crocker.)

Throughout his career the singer dispensed hundred-dollar bills like matchbooks. "I found him to be very professional, very exacting, and very generous," says Lee Hazen, a recording engineer who got his first break when he was hired in 1966 to run the studio at Syd Nathan's King Records in Cincinnati, Brown's recording home for the first fifteen years of his career. Hazen supervised the sessions for Brown's first Christmas album. "He tipped me a hundred-dollar bill at the end of each session," he says. "That was a week's pay back then."

James Spencer was a freelance photographer who mustered a career in Harlem by befriending such photogenic luminaries as Muhammad Ali and Malcolm X. When he took some photos of Brown onstage at the Apollo, Brown instructed Bobbit, his manager and an old Nation of Islam associate of Spencer's, to pay the man an unsolicited five hundred dollars. Brown "kept a wad of cash in his pocket, and he'd flip out some bills on the street," says Wayne Cochran, a contemporary who modeled his "White Knight of Soul" act on the *Live at the Apollo* album. "He'd see young black guys on the streets, see that they had no sense of destiny, of dreams. His political views grew out of that."

In 1969, *Look* magazine estimated Brown's income for the previous year at two and a half million dollars, ten percent of which was said to have been earmarked for youth groups and other charities. For most of his life the singer played Santa—"Santa Claus Goes Straight to the Ghetto," as one of his funkiest Christmas tunes implored—often touring the old neighborhood in Augusta in his limousine during the holidays, handing out turkeys and toys. Even the notorious fine money he collected from his musicians ultimately went to a good cause, according to Joe Dupars, the trumpeter on "Papa's Got a Brand New Bag" and "Cold Sweat." "I've never heard nobody say this," says Dupars. "He took the fine money and gave us a party around Christmastime. That's where that money went."

If money, in Brown's mind, was the one resource that would ensure personal pride and well-being, he had allies. In the last years of his life, Martin Luther King campaigned for jobs, equal opportunity employment, and a guaranteed minimum income for the lowest classes of Americans. Achieving an end to Jim Crow discrimination had not been enough, King argued. "I worked to get these people the right to eat hamburgers," the reverend told Bayard Rustin, "and now I've got to do something . . . to help them get the money to buy them."

"To be a poor man is hard," wrote W. E. B. Du Bois in *The Souls of Black Folk*, "but to be a poor race in a land of dollars is the very bottom of hardships." If James Brown measured his own worth by the size of his concert grosses, he also took great satisfaction in the belief that he was modeling a dream of financial security for his core constituents—the ordinary working-class people who saved for weeks to indulge themselves in the sacred ritual of the James Brown Revue, just as Bishop Daddy Grace's worshipers typically filled the coffers with more money than they could afford. "I'm a racist when it comes to freedom," Brown once said. "I can't rest until the black man in America is let out of jail, until his dollar's as good as the next man's."

In that era of two- and three-a-day shows, winning fans in fickle markets was the equivalent of hand-to-hand combat—

methodical, unpredictable, and fraught with high costs. For entertainers with sufficient charisma, television was, by contrast, an H-bomb of efficiency. In 1961 Brown began making appearances on Dick Clark's *American Bandstand*, which was making stars of everyone who appeared on the show. From there, Brown soon became a regular guest on *Where the Action Is*, a West Coast pop showcase also produced by Clark. The host of the program was Steve Alaimo, a onetime teen idol whose relationship with Clark went back to the late 1950s, when Alaimo's Miami band served as backing musicians for Clark's Caravan of Stars tour.

Even more potent was *The T.A.M.I. Show*, a one-off concert event held at the Santa Monica Civic Auditorium in October 1964. Music director Jack Nitzsche and young director Steve Binder (who would go on to oversee the career-rescuing television special for Elvis Presley known as the " '68 Comeback") assembled a lineup of pop luminaries, including the Beach Boys, Smokey Robinson and the Miracles, the Supremes, and the Rolling Stones. Brown's spectacular performance, crowing like an eagle and dancing like a hummingbird, set the audience into a frenzy. *T.A.M.I.*, which was screened in movie theaters around the country, was a first encounter with the consummate showman for many fans of acts such as Lesley Gore and Jan and Dean, and Brown made the most of it.

Prefigured by the slippery "Out of Sight," two songs released in 1965 boosted Brown once and for all into the company of the pop music elite. "Papa's Got a Brand New Bag, Pt. 1," issued as a King single in July 1965, was an edited version of a hypnotic, nearly seven-minute experiment in bop commercialism ("Pts. 1, 2 & 3") recorded in February. Cropped to two minutes and six seconds, the song was mastered at a slightly accelerated pace, effectively fortifying the original session. On paper, the song leaned on some of Brown's, and R&B's, old gambits—the repetitive, trainlike horn blurts, the singer's recitation of dance moves ("Papa, he doin' the Jerk / He's doin' the Twist, just like this / He's doin' the fight, every day and every night"). In execution, however, the song, with its herky-jerky rhythm and a stop-time chorus that was the perfect cue for the singer to break out one of his show-stopping moves, was the genesis of a new style of music. "It's a little beyond me right now," Brown admitted to a young Alan Leeds, an avid admirer who had landed a radio interview with the star. "I'm actually fightin' the future. . . . Take any record off your stack and put it on your box, even a James Brown record, and you won't find one that sounds like this one. It's a new bag, just like I sang."

Part of the key to Brown's new direction was the growing influence of bop within the group, as more theory-trained musicians—Joe Dupars, Nat Jones, Waymon Reed—began to enter the circle. If the hard bop of the 1950s and early '60s suppressed the monasticism of bebop in favor of a rawer form of expression, that expression often came from a distinctly black perspective. Rooted in gospel and blues, hard bop was, as author David Rosenthal wrote, "sometimes bleak, often tormented, but always cathartic; and it was 'bad' (sinister, menacing) in the sense that James Brown was 'bad.'" So-called soul-jazz, epitomized by bandleaders such as the organist Jimmy Smith and the saxophonist Lee Morgan, was often consciously formulated with jukeboxes, dance floors, and potential pop crossover in mind. Just as some of these musicians were looking toward James Brown, he was looking right back. His instrumental records of the time, if largely forgettable—not least because Brown himself often played the lead on organ, despite his almost complete lack of training—were typically tilted toward the soul-jazz market. Brown's vocal music, too, was reflecting that shifting sensibility. As drummer and bandleader Art Blakey once described, "Fire! That's what people want. You know, music is supposed to wash away the dust of everyday life. . . . You don't just play out of the top of your head, or play down to the people. I think you should play *to* the people."

"Papa" was closely followed by "I Got You (I Feel Good)," a reworked version of a song that had been in the repertoire since early 1962, when King released a single called "I Found You" by protégé Yvonne Fair, one of Brown's first female counterparts (and companions; out of wedlock, she would soon give birth to a son for Brown). With its subtle rumba beat and its slightly tipsy horns, Fair's original version could have passed as a product of the cosmopolitan New Orleans arranger Allen Toussaint. Back in Brown's hands, recorded as "I Got You" in late 1964 and intended for release on Smash, the arrangement was slinkier, a bit closer to the vest. Entangled in the legal troubles between Brown and King, the song wasn't released in its euphoric final form until November 1965.

"Brand New Bag," a number-one R&B hit for eight weeks in the summer of 1965, reached number eight on the pop top forty. "I Got You," which sat on top of the R&B chart for six weeks, outdid its predecessor with pop audiences, capping off at number three, Brown's best showing to date and, in fact, the best pop statistic of his entire career. (Incredibly, although he would log seventeen number-one R&B hits and place forty-four songs in the top forty over the course of his career, James Brown never had a number-one pop hit.)

By 1966, though, he knew he finally had their attention. The youth music of the 1950s and early '60s was maturing into social consciousness, and Brown, already in his thirties and a father several times over, sensed an opportunity to present himself as a role model. Holding himself up as an exemplar not only fed his considerable ego and his genuine desire to help others—it seemed like potentially good business, too. When Motown released a recording of Martin Luther King's "Great March to Freedom" speech, founder Berry Gordy made a sales pitch: "This album belongs in the home of every American and should be required listening for every American child, white or black."

To Brown, all of his records were required listening. Now he was ready to prove it. Recorded in August and released in October of '66, "Don't Be a Dropout" was the singer's first real "message" song. It was not the most artful message: "Without an education, you might as well be dead," he sang, accompanied by shrill horns and an unwavering 4/4 beat. But self-improvement was a message that hit him close to home. "I'm a dropout," as he told *Jet*, "and it hurts."

On a visit to Oakland to play Sweet's Ballroom in 1964, Brown had caught a local television forum featuring a bright young Berkeley-trained lawyer named Donald Warden. Warden, a philosophy major from Howard University who had applied to Berkeley after becoming intrigued by the San Francisco Beat writers, was one of the founders of a group called the Afro-American Association, which focused on black history and community development. Among the participants were future Black Panthers Bobby Seale and Huey Newton, future U.S. District Court Senior Judge Thelton Henderson, and future U.S. congressman and Oakland Mayor Ron Dellums. The

AAA preached messages of unity, self-help, education, and dignity. The slogan on their insignia read "Each One Teach Two." They ran a multifaceted business operation called Dignity Enterprises, which featured a print shop and a women's clothing manufacturing operation, among other ventures. One member, Ed Howard, was a draftsman at Kaiser Engineers, where he convinced management to open up its hiring practices to local African-Americans.

Warden was essentially the group's public mouthpiece, hosting a weekly radio program on KDIA and, later, a local television show called *Black Dignity*. On the radio, he began to attract visiting entertainers, such as Aretha Franklin and Ike and Tina Turner. When Brown saw Warden on television discussing the critical importance of education, he sent word that he wanted to meet the young lawyer. "He said, 'What you said, I feel it,' " recalls Warden, now Dr. Khalid Abdullah Tariq Al-Mansour. " 'I can't articulate it, but I feel it.' I said, 'Brother, you're the key. I'm just the gatekeeper. You have the masses.' "

For some time the members of the AAA had been debating how to recruit popular musicians into their movement. In the eyes of the Afro-American Association, underachievers had no excuses. Members sometimes demonstrated outside schools, chanting, "No dropouts. No flunk-outs. Honor grades will make you feel like a black man should." Now Brown began a dialogue with the group, and with Warden in particular, that would continue through the rest of the decade. "That was one of the things I most wanted to do through my music—to teach Black people how to very nicely say . . . 'I'm too strong,' " as Brown would recall. "I wanted us to be brought in, not shut out."

Warden and his colleagues were instrumental in helping the

singer bring ideas into his music. "I've always felt that the only thing to unite our race would be music," Warden said in the 1969 *Look* magazine cover story on Brown. "It seemed to me that James had taken the powerful, cathartic music of Africa and the gospel tradition and captured our youth. I told him, 'If you want to, you can be the next meaningful leader of our race.' "

In August 1965, Brown had been in Los Angeles, making appearances on *Where the Action Is* and *Shindig* and at a reception for the teen film *Ski Party*, in which he had a farcical cameo. When the Watts riots broke out, according to Joe Dupars, Brown took time out of his schedule to walk through the neighborhood. "James took that blowhorn and he walked the streets of Watts," Dupars recalls. "He said, 'Come on, let's do the right thing.' "

Almost exactly one year later, a few weeks before recording "Dropout," Brown was back in Los Angeles, spending a day touring government-funded Los Angeles recreation centers called Teen Posts. The visit was part of a citywide outreach program developed in the aftermath of the riots called Operation Cool Head. Together with Los Angeles Lakers basketball star Walt Hazard, the singer addressed local students, asking them to sign pledges of good citizenship and, in exchange, giving away copies of his records. The radio sponsor was KGFJ, home of Magnificent Montague, the soul DJ whose popular catch phrase for a hot record, "Burn, baby, burn!," had been adopted by looters during the previous summer's riots. When someone asked why the itinerary did not include any stops in Watts, a visit was quickly arranged, at the Westminster Neighborhood Association. A disc jockey announced the schedule change from the station's mobile unit, and a crowd of more than a thousand fans quickly gathered at the community center. Brown worked the assembly like a politician, smiling, shaking hands, and imploring his admirers to stay in school.

The singer sometimes claimed that he planned to sing "Don't Be a Dropout" on *The Ed Sullivan Show*, but that the host asked him not to. He first appeared on America's premier variety hour in early May, sharing the bill with the Supremes, the Robert Joffrey Ballet Company, the British comedian Billy Baxter, and a man demonstrating quick-draw gunplay, among others. Brown sang a brief medley of "Brand New Bag" and "I Got You" before returning later in the program to showcase his latest single, "It's a Man's Man's Man's World." The famously stodgy Sullivan, who had evidently scouted Brown himself at the Apollo, called him "young Jim Brown" and noted that the singer was a true Southerner—"picked cotton, worked in a coalyard." After Brown's typically electric performance of the medley (accompanied, at Brown's insistence, by his own band), Sullivan waved him over to take a bow, then offered viewers a languid assessment: "Boy, that is really excitement, isn't it?" Before the show Sullivan, still sensitive to prudish viewers almost a decade after the show's mythmaking Elvis Presley appearance, warned Brown against excessive gyrations. "But that's my act!" Brown protested. Despite the constraints, the singer knew precisely what a booking on *The Ed Sullivan Show* meant to his career. Sitting onstage after the show, he said to his bandmates, "Man, I have arrived."

Brown appeared again on the *Sullivan* show later in the year, performing "Prisoner of Love." "Don't Be a Dropout," even if it had been featured, likely was not destined for great impact. However commendable its social motive, the song was simply a mediocre James Brown offering. Though it reached number four

on the R&B chart—another indicator of Brown's utter dominance of the field—it failed to crack the pop top forty.

For Brown, however, it was not just empty sloganeering. If
there was one thing this supremely self-confident man found
himself self-conscious about, it was his seventh-grade education.
He mentioned it throughout his life as the primary obstacle he
had to overcome in his pursuit of stardom. In addition to such
giveaways such as coats and bicycles, he began awarding some
fans five-hundred-dollar scholarships to regional black colleges.

Brown's newfound commitment to education earned him
his first taste of national politics. In Washington, D.C., he introduced "Don't Be a Dropout" at an Urban League rally and
presented Vice President Hubert Humphrey with the first copy
of the single. In turn, Humphrey named Brown chairman of
the recording artists' committee of the government's new "Stay
in School" campaign. (Brown and Muhammad Ali had been
chosen to co-chair the Johnson administration's proposed youth
outreach program, but the offer to Ali was rescinded amid the
controversy over his refusal to serve in the military as a consci-
entious objector.) In the coming months, the singer would give
away thousands of buttons that read "Stay in School."

Never one to squander an opportunity, it's likely Brown knew
that the vice president was also working with Stax, the Memphis record company then providing some of his stiffest competition among soul music fans. In early 1967 Stax sent out a
promotional album to radio stations around the country, with
songs and messages from such roster notables as Otis Redding,
Carla Thomas, and Sam & Dave, urging listeners to heed their
studies. Humphrey wrote a letter that ran as the liner notes for
the *Stay in School* compilation. In it, he noted that machines

were eliminating more and more jobs for unskilled laborers. "That high school diploma could mean the difference between a real future and a mere existence. . . . My young friends, that's where the action is!!!" It was not an especially popular message. In Memphis, where the marquee lettering on the old movie theater that housed the Stax offices was briefly changed from SOULSVILLE, U.S.A. to STAY IN SCHOOL, neighborhood kids threw rocks at the sign.

Though Brown's eventual support of Humphrey in the 1968 presidential campaign is sometimes noted as a misstep, in truth the vice president, nicknamed the "Happy Warrior," had a long and distinguished history of advocacy for civil rights. As mayor of Minneapolis, he first came to national prominence during the 1948 Democratic National Convention, when he spearheaded an effort by progressive Democrats to force the issue. "To those who say that we are rushing this issue of civil rights, I say to them we are a hundred and seventy-two years too late!" he cried. It was time, he argued, for the Democratic Party "to get out of the shadow of states' rights and walk forthrightly into the bright sunshine of human rights." When the Democrats narrowly adopted the civil rights platform, what they lost by alienating the so-called Dixiecrats (who formed their own party, nominating Senator Strom Thurmond for president), they regained through the support of African-Americans. The black vote, it has been argued, may have been the deciding factor in President Harry S. Truman's upset reelection over favored Republican challenger Thomas E. Dewey.

Brown's interaction with the vice president did not mark his introduction to the political arena. That had come a few months earlier, in support of the activist James Meredith. In June 1966, various factions of the splintering civil rights movement converged on Memphis, where Meredith lay recuperating in the hospital. Meredith, the Air Force veteran who had integrated Ole Miss, the University of Mississippi, in 1962 under heavy National Guard protection, was shot in the back on the sixth of June as he set out on the first leg of his symbolic "March Against Fear" from Memphis to Jackson. The march had been planned to symbolize the rights of black Americans to travel without impediment through the Deep South.

In a strained atmosphere, movement organizers jockeyed for position in Memphis. Dr. Martin Luther King headed the contingent from the SCLC. Floyd McKissick was there as the new leader of CORE, having supplanted the outgoing co-founder of the group, James Farmer. Roy Wilkins of the NAACP and Whitney Young of the National Urban League flew in. And an emerging figure in SNCC, a Bronx-schooled Trinidadian named Stokely Carmichael, was about to claim center stage in the civil rights struggle.

A few days after visiting Meredith in the hospital, Carmichael was among those arrested in Greenwood, Mississippi, as protesters attempted to press on with the wounded man's march. In a subsequent speech, Carmichael called for a new attitude for the civil rights movement, which was beginning to fracture under the weight of one disillusioning crisis after another. "This is the twenty-seventh time that I've been arrested," Carmichael said. "I ain't going to jail no more. The only way we gonna stop them white men from whuppin' us is to take over. What we gonna start saying now is Black Power!"

The phrase, as Peniel E. Joseph points out in *Waiting 'Til the*

Midnight Hour: A Narrative History of Black Power in America, did not spring to life at that moment. It had been referenced in the past by such black activists as Powell, the actor Paul Robeson, and the novelist Richard Wright. In the summer of 1966, however, those two words reconfigured the entire framework of the civil rights movement. More conciliatory leaders such as Wilkins and Young, who tried in vain to get the marchers to use the event as an opportunity to voice support for President Johnson's latest civil rights initiative, pulled out of the Meredith March in protest. But King, the apostle of nonviolence, was by this time coming to the realization that he needed to foster a "coalition of conscience," one that would actively seek the inclusion of the radical left, for the movement to continue.

In late June, as the march was scheduled to arrive in Jackson, a rally was planned on the campus of Tougaloo College, on the city's northern outskirts. Around the woody grounds of the campus, various factions of the movement claimed space for themselves and debated how best to have their respective agendas heard. The comedian and activist Dick Gregory, whose autobiography, *Nigger,* had been a publishing phenomenon in 1964, served as liaison between the factions as well as host of the rally. The open-air assemblage drew between ten and twenty thousand supporters. Burt Lancaster and Marlon Brando arrived, and spoke. Harry Belafonte, Tony Bennett, and Olympic hero Rafer Johnson took part; Sammy Davis, Jr., wearing the humble denim jacket of the movement's field workers, sang two songs without musical accompaniment. But among these celebrities, each already noted for his civil rights activism, James Brown was the sole featured performer. With the stage so crowded "one could hardly tell the performers from the audience," according to *Jet* magazine, Brown, wearing a tight black suit and a ruffled, unbuttoned blue shirt, followed SNCC program director Cleveland Sellers to the stage. The bearded Sellers, the magazine reported, parted the crowd for Brown "like Moses." Brown addressed the crowd during his brief set, which featured "I Got You (I Feel Good)" and "Try Me," remarking about how brave a man Meredith was, that he respected what he did. Before leaving, Brown, *Jet* reported, contributed a thousand dollars to help defray the cost of the march.

Sellers had known Brown since 1964, when the civil rights advocate called Brown in his hotel room in Atlanta and introduced himself to his fellow South Carolina native. Meeting in person, Brown listened with interest as the young activist explained the aims of the upcoming Mississippi Freedom Summer project. When the singer told Sellers he'd help any way he could, Sellers suggested he buy dinner for some of his colleagues. For the next few years, the two men cultivated a relationship; whenever their paths crossed, Brown would treat a group of volunteers to a meal and backstage passes. It was, recalls Sellers, a welcome morale boost. In exchange, Brown asked for access to Dr. King, and on several occasions Sellers helped facilitate private conversations between the two men.

"It wasn't public," says Sellers. "The people inside the movement knew about my relationship to him."

Brown's political engagement after Meredith's shooting was precisely the kind of response the activist had been hoping to compel, says Meredith, who still lives in Jackson. "I felt that was their responsibility," he says of the entertainers who became engaged as a result of his symbolic protest. "The whole purpose of starting the march was to get the focus to where it could be made known that this was everybody's business. As far as I know, this was the first time James Brown had actually understood or moved in that direction." Brown and Meredith would remain on cordial terms, with the singer asking the activist to appear at several of his fund-raising concerts over the years.

By attempting to "take back the movement," Meredith's aim was to expose what he saw as the fatal flaw in King's doctrine of nonviolence. In the *New York Times* just after the shooting, he'd made the point clear, saying he regretted the fact that he had been unarmed at the time of the attack. "Who the hell ever said I was nonviolent?" he'd been quoted. "I spent eight years in the military and the rest of my life in Mississippi."

After the marchers in Mississippi made Carmichael's "Black Power" a rallying cry, Vice President Humphrey denounced the phrase in an address at the fifty-seventh annual convention of the NAACP. "Racism is racism," he said, "and there is no room in America for racism of any color. And we must reject calls for racism, whether they come from a throat that is white or one that is black." Brown instinctively felt that the phrase "Black Power" would be polarizing. "To some people it meant black pride and black people owning businesses and having a voice in politics," as he wrote in his autobiography. "That's what it meant to me. To other people it meant self-defense against attacks like the one on Meredith. But to others it meant a revolutionary bag."

For King, the Meredith March was also momentous, if unsettling. Even as he despaired over the movement's infighting, he managed to deliver one of the speeches that would define his legacy. Having already appealed to white Americans to consider the devastating psychological impact of black neglect—"When you are forever fighting a degenerating sense of 'nobodiness,' " he wrote in his famous "Letter from Birmingham Jail" in 1963, "then you will understand why we find it difficult to wait"—he called for the abolition of such "nobodiness" in his address in Greenwood. "You are *somebody*," he thundered to the crowd. "I want every one of you to say that out loud now to yourself—'I am somebody.' "

The mid-1960s were the heyday of protest music, with Joan Baez and Peter, Paul and Mary performing at the March on Washington, Barry McGuire's "Eve of Destruction" reaching number one in the summer of 1965, even the no-longer-boyish Beatles entering their phase of social commentary. Soul singers were beginning to find their own political footing, too, led by the maturing child star Stevie Wonder, who recorded a version of Bob Dylan's "Blowin' in the Wind" and imagined "A Place in the Sun" for people of all colors. Another Motown artist, Marvin Gaye, found himself sickened when he heard one of his own love songs interrupted by news of the outbreak of the Watts riots. "I wanted to throw the radio down and burn all the bullshit songs I'd been singing and get out there and kick ass with the rest of the brothers," he recalled. Martha and the Vandellas' "Dancing in the Streets" became a popular soundtrack to episodes of urban unrest, and Aretha Franklin's "Respect" was interpreted as a claim to dignity as racially attuned as it was about gender. The impact of such songs was impressive. "You'd hear Aretha three or four times an hour," as Gregory once remarked. "You'd only hear [Dr.] King on the news."

Topical music was never before so commercially oriented. As a folk tradition, however, it had always been an effective method of political dissemination. "A pamphlet, no matter how good, is never read more than once," as the union organizer Joe Hill once said, "but a song is learned by heart and repeated over and over." With revolution, or at least some major changes, in the air, James Brown began to address his songs not to an object of romantic attraction but a collective audience. With the civil rights movement cracking into a kaleidoscope of opinions and Vietnam threatening to create an unbridgeable gulf between left and right, he saw a country mired in animosities and implored his constituents, as 1967 came to a close, to "Get It Together."

Brown's emerging topicality coincided with a major leap forward for the music itself, as the band developed the rhythmic swing and swagger that would come to be known as funk. Funk was to R&B what Wilt Chamberlain's finger roll was to the set shot—the natural elevation of an existing skill set. With Nat Jones's brief tenure as bandleader producing "Brand New Bag," "I Got You," "Ain't That a Groove," and other tunes that plotted the course, newcomer Pee Wee Ellis was the next critical component in Brown's virtual invention of funk music. When Jones, a former high school band instructor, abruptly quit the band, suffering from psychological problems that would keep him institutionalized for much of his life, Ellis proved amply ready to begin writing the arrangements.

If James Brown was audacious, his band members were increasingly quick to pick up the cue, goading one another to new feats of interactivity. Each of the drummers, and there were many—Melvin Parker, Clyde Stubblefield, Bernard Purdie, John "Jabo" Starks—contributed their own brand of interpretive syncopation. The ever-growing horn section, meanwhile, combined precisely coordinated lyric phrases with plenty of open space cleared out for boppish improvisation. Ellis, for instance, wrote "Cold Sweat" on a scrap of paper on the bus after listening to

Brown wordlessly describe a fragment of an idea he had for a new tune. The riff, as the arranger points out, was directly influenced by Miles Davis's "So What."

Ellis had grown up on bebop and hard bop—Charlie Parker, Dizzy Gillespie, Benny Golson, Gene Ammons, Art Blakey. As Nat Jones had helped Brown move his instrumental releases beyond novelties and dance crazes, Ellis pushed further toward sophisticated, relentlessly swinging exercises in meter and extemporization. Ellis received writing or co-writing credits for several of them, including "The Chicken," which was later adopted as a signature tune by the jazz-bass virtuoso Jaco Pastorius.

Band members who shared Ellis's jazz training included Waymon Reed, the trumpeter who had recruited the new arranger; trumpeter Joe Dupars, whose impressive résumé features work with Aretha Franklin, the Isley Brothers, and a long stint on the road with Wilson Pickett; and trombonist Fred Wesley, who was suitably flabbergasted upon joining in early 1968. "I got the sense that James was plugged into the band, and it was generating energy directly to his body," he would recall.

As the songs grew longer and more vamp-oriented under Ellis's musical direction, they were increasingly inundated with the verbal projectiles for which Brown remains famous—the war whoops, the husky "Good God!"'s, the diaphragmatic grunts of a man throwing off a heavy burden. Like the forceful heave— "White man tells me . . . hunh . . . Damn yo' soul"—of the folk poet Sterling Brown in his debut collection, *Southern Road* (1933), such exclamations are rooted in the rhythms of laborers and chain gangs. Yet "the 'hunh' that punctuates the poem is more than an involuntary accompaniment to the prisoner's physical exertion," as the authors of *Spoken Soul* explain. "It's

★ Boston mayor Kevin White and James Brown, onstage at the Boston Garden, April 5, 1968. *Courtesy of WGBH Educational Foundation.* © *1968 WGBH/ Boston*

★ The old Boston Garden, circa 1968. *Courtesy of The Sports Museum, Boston, MA*

★ Poster from Brown's previous Boston Garden appearance, photographed in Roxbury. © *Steve Nelson*

★ Dr. Martin Luther King, Jr., with then Massachusetts secretary of state Kevin White, April 1965. © Boston Herald

★ Tom Atkins campaigning for the Boston City Council, 1967. © Boston Herald

★ Brown after a costume change, Boston Garden.
© The Boston Globe/*Landov*

★ Duke Ellington performing on *The Ed Sullivan Show*, 1959.
© CBS/*Landov*

★ Bishop Charles Manuel "Sweet Daddy" Grace, founder of the United House of Prayer for All People. "He was like a god on Earth," Brown recalled.
Courtesy of the Kirn Memorial Library (Sargeant Memorial Room), Norfolk, VA

★ Brown signing autographs in London, 1966. Behind him is his manager, Ben Bart. © *EMPICS/Landov*

★ Vice President Hubert Humphrey and Brown discuss the singer's new song, "Don't Be a Dropout," 1966. *Courtesy of Alan Leeds*

★ Left to right: Dr. Martin Luther King, Jr., James Meredith, Stokely Carmichael, and Floyd McKissick continue the "Meredith March" for freedom, June 1966. © *Topham/The Image Works*

★ SNCC program director Cleveland Sellers, who arranged Brown's meetings with Dr. Martin Luther King, Jr., is interviewed by a reporter after refusing induction into the army in Atlanta, May 1967. Behind Sellers is SNCC chairman Stokely Carmichael. © Associated Press

★ Protesters during the Memphis sanitation workers strike, 1968. *Courtesy of Walter P. Reuther Library, Wayne State University, Richard L. Copley, photographer*

★ James Brown greets soldiers in Vietnam, 1968. © *The Everett Collection*

★ Brown onstage with Cincinnati band the Dapps, 1968. *Courtesy of Bob Patton*

★ Brown in Las Vegas, circa 1969. *Photofest, Inc.*

★ Brown unwinds after a performance, West Palm Beach, 1970. With him is promotions man Bob Patton. *Courtesy of Bob Patton*

★ A young Rev. Al Sharpton presents James Brown with a "Black Record" award, 1974. © *James Spencer*

★ Brown spars with his fellow cultural ambassador, heavyweight champ Muhammad Ali. © *Topham/The Image Works*

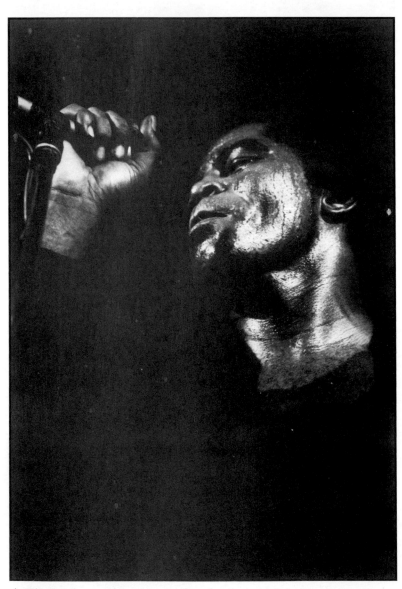

★ The hardest working man in show business. *Photofest, Inc.*

a scoff, a jeer, a private word passed between Brown [the poet] and his black reader, a remark that recalls the energetic 'hunh' of black preachers at the height of their sermons and simultaneously takes a jab at the presumptions of white folks."

James Brown—secular preacher, onetime jailbird, undeniable sexual being—needed no linguist to teach him the meaning of exclamation. "James Brown said, 'I'm gonna express myself in a raw, untamed way,' " as Al Sharpton once recalled. Most entertainers, Sharpton observed, want to be accepted. "James Brown wanted to be *felt*. And his scream, his moan, his groan, all of that, was 'I want to express myself even if you're not comfortable with it. I have to release this.' And when he released it, he released a scream in all of us that had so much scream built up in us but never had the nerve to let it go." That scream, by the mid-1960s, was newly meaningful amid the pent-up frustrations of the civil rights movement.

Beginning, slowly but surely, in the 1950s, black Americans were rising to unprecedented prominence in American life, with symbolic advances by representatives of Du Bois's "talented tenth" in the dramatic arts, business, and public service. But even after Little Rock, the lunch counter sit-ins, and the March on Washington, rare still were the instances in which talent could overcome white America's lingering expectation of servility from the "Negro" underclass. In the early years of the 1960s, larger-than-life, unapologetically successful African-Americans remained few and far between. The political sphere had Adam Clayton Powell, the flamboyant congressman from Harlem who flaunted a decadent lifestyle and compelled supporters to "Keep the faith, baby!" The sporting world had seen the recent emergence of Muhammad Ali, the brash heavyweight champion given a new name by Nation of Islam leader Elijah Muhammad. And the openly gay novelist and essayist James Baldwin made the cover of *Time* in 1963 upon the publication of his provocative essay collection *The Fire Next Time*. Largely, however, black celebrities were much more likely to be awarded the spotlight with less confrontational personae than men such as these. As the poet Nikki Giovanni would write, ominously, in her piece, "Reflections on April 4, 1968": "The question—does it have rhythm? The answer—yes. The response—kill it."

The whole Brown package—the singer's physical exertion and hip vernacular, the raucous brass voices filling the places where backup singers would once have crooned, the radical emphasis on syncopation and musical space—amounted to a brand-new style of music. The descriptive term "funky" had been part of black culture for decades. Robert Farris Thompson, longstanding scholar of African-American art and music at Yale, has suggested that it may have originated with the Bantu-language phrase *lu-fuki*, or "positive sweat." As Robert Palmer pointed out in *Rock & Roll: An Unruly History*, here was a very plausible, if unconscious, birthplace for Brown's "Cold Sweat"—arguably the Ground Zero of funk—which reached number seven on the pop chart in the extrasensory summer of 1967 and was Ellis's true coming-of-age as Brown's musical director.

Fellow musicians were in awe. " 'Cold Sweat' deeply affected the musicians I knew," said Atlantic Records producer Jerry Wexler. "It just freaked them out. For a time, no one could get a handle on what to do next." Renowned conductor Michael Tilson Thomas has remarked that even classical students were studying Brown's new bag: "You could use your ears to go down inside the music and explore all the amazing levels it had," he said. "In those years, we were playing Boulez and Stravinsky, but we were listening to James Brown."

But while Jones and Ellis brought fortuitous wrinkles to the sound of the James Brown bands of the time, it was Brown himself, with his overwhelming personality, who unmistakably commanded the music. "Anybody who says James Brown is nothing without the band is wrong," says Fred Wesley. "Any band that James Brown sat in front of was *the band*." When the original J.B.s, the prolific but short-lived band that backed Brown in 1970 and early '71, decamped for George Clinton's Parliament-Funkadelic lineup, Wesley, one of the few accompanists to remain, was put in charge of assembling another new group. The recruits, says Wesley, were clearly inexperienced, and he was anxious about it: "I didn't know how James was going to react, because it was shaky. But when he got in front of it, started patting his foot, singing and snorting and carrying on, that band came together. The band came together right then and there, even though I had been rehearsing them for two weeks."

Always seeking the upper hand, Brown was one of the first major performers to understand the value of owning the rights to his own recordings and publishing. When in the mid-1960s he negotiated a new agreement with King Records, he demanded, and won, control over his master recordings, stuffing them in a bag and taking them on the road with him. Determined to leave as little room as possible for rivals to challenge his chart domination, he pumped an endless stream of recordings into the pipeline, often recycling castoff songs from long-forgotten sessions. (In this practice he was perfectly in tune with Syd Nathan, the irascible, crassly entrepreneurial founder of the

King label, with whom Brown would otherwise engage in never-ending debate over the artistic merit, and commercial viability, of the singer's material.)

Brown often used his songwriting credits as leverage, dangling them in front of associates in return for favors or, perhaps, the annulment of debts. Charles Bobbit, the personal manager who was with Brown until the day he died, is ascribed as co-writer on many of the singer's songs, and Bobbit is sole owner of the writing credit for "Give It Up or Turnit a Loose," recorded in 1968, just after he joined the organization. Several of Brown's mid-1960s recordings feature the name Bud Hobgood, an artist and repertoire man who worked for Syd Nathan. "People wondered for years—did Bud Hobgood have something on James?" as David Matthews, a jazz-trained arranger who worked on many sessions with Brown in the early 1970s, once said.

But offering his associates publishing credits was also Brown's way of imparting his hard-earned wisdom. "Soul Power, Pts. 1 & 2," for instance, recorded in January 1971, in Washington, D.C., was Fred Wesley's initiation as arranger. Brown offered his associate a choice: he could either take $125 or 25 percent of the publishing royalties. Wesley, who had just returned from California, needed a coat for the chilly East Coast weather, so he told his boss he would take the cash. Brown shook his head and said, "Son, I'm gonna tell you something. If you had taken the twenty-five percent, that'd take care of your family from now on.'" Wesley took the publishing every time thereafter.

"I don't know if he liked me," says Wesley. "But he did open my eyes. He gave enough [credits] to where it has taken care of families. I don't know if Pee Wee got all he was supposed to get, but I'm satisfied with what I got."

As much as he considered himself a churchgoing man, Brown's true religion was capitalism. It was "enterprise as emancipation," as Philip Gourevitch put it in a 2002 *New Yorker* profile, "ownership and tycoondom as the ultimate social justice." He tried his hand as a restaurateur and a nightclub owner (his short-lived food chain, launched in 1969 and likely inspired by Ali's own restaurant venture of the time, Champburger, was called Gold Platter). Recordings credited to individual band members and other protégés were "James Brown Productions." Like Julius Caesar, Brown even issued his own form of currency: Designed by members of the Afro-American Association to encourage black support of black business, the endeavor was called Black and Brown Trading Stamps. Brown was named a director, and the stamps featured the King of Soul's own likeness. "James Brown money," says Pee Wee Ellis with a chuckle. "I remember seeing these bills with James Brown's face. The ego of this guy!"

Brown saw himself as a builder of empire. At the start of 1968 he bought the first of his three radio stations, WGYW in Knoxville, Tennessee. His first order of business was to change the call letters to WJBE—James Brown Enterprises. The singer would soon add Baltimore's WEBB and Augusta's WRDW to the fold. The call letters WEBB, as the staff and listeners liked to joke, were shorthand for "We Enjoy Being Black." (That echoed the quip about Memphis's rhythm and blues powerhouse, WDIA, the first station to be programmed by African-Americans: "We Done Integrated Already.") The Augusta station was Brown's pride and joy. It was the same station outside of which he had shined shoes as a boy, a fact he never failed to note when asked about the remarkable arc of his life.

Of all the hundreds of black-oriented radio stations across the country, only two others besides Brown's had black ownership by the late 1960s. His own stations, Brown declared, would serve three major purposes. They would act as the voice of the black communities in their respective cities, they would help promote Brown's own emerging image as a symbol of African-American independence and business initiative, and they would provide a training ground for minority candidates wishing to break into the media world.

"I remember wearing one of his buttons as a young child in elementary school—'Say It Loud,'" says Tene Croom, who grew up in a proud, committed household in Knoxville. "He was outspoken in using his celebrity to get people to listen and to make change." Today, Croom is an award-winning journalist for American Urban Radio Networks. She began her career in radio at WJBE, working for James Brown.

"That," as the singer would recall years later, "was real black power."

★ ★ ★ 8 ★ ★ ★

THINGS GOT TO GET BETTER

The James Brown concert flickered into living rooms across the greater Boston area the only way it could have—in black and white. Though television was in the midst of the transition to color programming in 1968, the cables in place at the old Boston Garden were for black-and-white transmission. There was no time to lay color cable, so WGBH brought three of its old, cumbersome RCA TK-60 cameras, which were, in the words of producer Russ Morash, "as big as easy chairs."

The rough, dim footage wasn't the only factor that gave the broadcast an air of mystery. Brown, at the outset a bit more contained than usual, squinted through the conical spotlight that encircled his microphone stand from above. His broad forehead shone with perspiration; the wax in his chiseled pompadour glistened. Behind the singer, the anonymity of his supporting musicians, cloaked in smoky shadows, added to the show's eerie aura.

From the reverse shot behind the stage, over Brown's right shoulder, the crowd is equally obscured by darkness. Though small in number, they're loud, of course—this is, after all, a James Brown show. But their hollers are distant, disembodied. There's a distinct impression throughout much of the concert that Brown is alone. He's searching for the way forward. The haze is thick; the arena is poorly lit. Periodic camera flashes from beyond the murk seem to blind the singer. Two months later, flying in helicopters at night in Vietnam, he would note the terrible beauty of the enemy's tracer bullets: "It was kind of pretty, if you didn't think they were meant to kill you."

To this day Morash, the producer, has a difficult time reviewing the grainy footage, which was recorded on open-reel videotape. (Film was prohibitively costly at the time.) "The cameras of the period were not as good as the merest surveillance camera in a 7-Eleven today," he says.

Still, Brown's incandescence burns through the gloom. After being spelled by Bobby Byrd, who muscles through cover versions of some of the past year's biggest non-Brown soul hits—Sam & Dave's "Soul Man," Wilson Pickett's "Mustang Sally," Arthur Conley's "Sweet Soul Music" ("Spotlight on James Brown, y'all / He's the king of them all, y'all")—Soul Brother Number One reappears in a form-fitting pullover, elbows bent, palms down, feeling his way into the nightly rendition of "It's a Man's Man's Man's World." The stark song, deliberately soured by the plucking and bowing of the band's unseen string trio, soon opens into a jazzy interlude echoing Dave Brubeck's timeless "Take Five." The singer drops to his knees as he reminds the audience of his shrill 1961 hit "Lost Someone," then wails a snatch from "Bewildered." With a sudden right cross thrown in the direction of the drum kit, he jolts the band into the climax of Percy Sledge's "When a Man Loves a Woman." No buildup, no progression— it's all payoff. *"When a man . . ."* Brown screeches, twisting his torso as he throws himself into the delivery, leaving the rest of the lyric to hang. Then he slips offstage.

"James . . . Brown . . . will . . . be back!" booms Maceo Parker.

The next set is Marva's. In early 1968, Marva Whitney was the featured female singer in the James Brown Revue. There had been many others. There was Bea Ford, Joe Tex's ex; the blues belter Etta James, briefly; Yvonne Fair, who introduced the song that would become "I Got You (I Feel Good)." Philadelphian Tammy Montgomery had a tempestuous nine-month stint with Brown before her reinvention with Motown, where she became Tammi Terrell, Marvin Gaye's ill-fated duet partner.

But Whitney, who was possessed of an especially knifelike singing voice, naturally complemented Brown. Born Marva Ann Manning, a onetime child performer with her family's group, the Manning Gospel Singers, she was plucked from her native Kansas City after the 1966 show there that had ended in rioting. When the Revue was on the road, she doubled as traveling secretary. (Many of Brown's musicians had downtime assignments. Both bassist Bernard Odum and valve trombonist Levi Raspbury, for instance, dropped in and out of the performing lineup as they logged long hours driving the bus or the equipment truck. "I did it all," as Clayton Fillyau, the influential drummer from the first *Live at the Apollo* album told author Jim Payne, "from playin' drums to truck drivin', bus drivin', road manager, and light technician.")

At the Boston Garden, as with all the shows she would participate in before her departure at the end of the decade, Whitney fulfilled the female version of Bobby Byrd's human jukebox act. She began with Etta James's recent hit "Tell Mama." Looking like a Supreme in a bouffant wig and a knee-length cocktail dress, the singer pledged to ease her listeners' troubles: "Tell Mama what's wrong, and I'll make everything all right." But her expression was unsmiling, anxious; on this night, those lyrics were a hard sell. She tried to expel her apprehension physically, by shouting, as she'd been taught by her mentor. Her set included versions of Aretha's "Chain of Fools," Gladys Knight's "I Heard It Through the Grapevine," and "You Better Check Yourself," a recent release by the Soul Brothers Six, a modestly successful group from Rochester, New York, Pee Wee Ellis's hometown, that was briefly signed to Atlantic Records.

After "Tell Mama," the accusatory tone shared by the other songs in Whitney's repertoire may well have represented her sticky personal situation with the star of the show. "I think she was the strongest of all my girlfriends," Brown would remember. But on this night, the songs she sang felt like broader message songs. Their common theme revolved around the betrayal of promises.

Whitney would go on to record some of Brown's most focused attempts at direct social engagement. "Things Got to Get Better (Get Together)," recorded in late April at King Studios in Cincinnati, was a classic double entendre—a romantic complaint that could also be heard as a call for social conciliation. A year later, she would have her biggest hit with "It's My Thing (You Can't Tell Me Who to Sock It To)," a feminist answer to the Isley Brothers hit, and she would release the self-explanatory advice song "You Got to Have a Job (If You Don't Work—You Don't Eat)," with Brown as duet partner.

In September 1968, five months after the Boston Garden appearance, Whitney recorded a vocal for an impromptu track the band had laid down at the Memorial Auditorium gig in Dallas the month before. The writing of the song, called "I'm Tired, I'm Tired, I'm Tired (Things Better Change Before It's Too Late)," is solely credited to Brown, and his influence, as ever, is transparent. But the material seems unusually somber. Whitney is tired of watching her man, her mother, her father all beaten down by life. "We can't let history repeat itself, can't let it take us back a hundred years," she sings. It's a gospel lament disguised, instrumentally, as a funky workout. The true reason for her despondency, she reveals just before the fadeout, is the death of Dr. King. "Can't take no more, y'all," she sings.

After the murder of Dr. King, Brown's songs began to demand engagement: "Say It Loud—I'm Black and I'm Proud." "Get Up, Get Into It, and Get Involved." "I Don't Want Nobody to Give Me Nothing (Open Up the Door I'll Get It Myself)." Like the essential demand for recognition seen on so many signs during the sanitation workers' strike in Memphis—"I Am a Man!"— Brown's music was soon inundated with similar sloganeering. Over the next several years James Brown Productions would release a steady diet of socially aware funk songs, often with one of the band members or featured acts as the credited artist—Fred Wesley and the J.B.s' "Damn Right I Am Somebody," for instance, which echoed both King and his associate, Jesse Jackson. Brown "took a lot of credit for things other people said, but he said it on a record," says Wesley. "He said it *louder*."

"Stand up and be a man," urged Bobby Byrd on "Sayin' It and Doin' It Are Two Different Things." Brown's move at the start of the new decade from King Records to the German-based Polydor label, a division of Deutsche Grammophon, included a provision for him to set up his own imprint. The People label would release tracks by the J.B.s and others with titles such as "Stand Up and Be Counted," "Blessed Blackness," and "The Soul of a Black Man." There were party songs about Watergate, paying taxes, the gas crisis.

According to Al Sharpton, Brown liked to put out his message records on the label he owned because he felt part of the message was black ownership. The intention, says Sharpton, was twofold—to politicize Brown's own label, and to draw attention to it by working to keep his own records commercially viable. While many of his releases were themselves socially driven—the original "Soul Power," for instance, or "Get Up, Get Into It, and Get Involved," or the eccentric anti-drug diatribe "King Heroin"—plenty more were, as the song said, unabashed "Escape-ism." In the 1970s, a decade in which many Americans would turn to hedonistic disengagement as a last resort of political protest, Brown celebrated the relaxation of sexual standards with songs such as "Hot Pants," "Get Up (I Feel Like Being a) Sex Machine)," and "I Got Ants in My Pants."

Like Whitney and Wesley, Hank Ballard was another member of the circle who carried out Brown's political notions. Nineteen sixty-nine's "Blackenized" essentially set to music Brown's newly composed rap on the differences between Negroes, colored people, and blacks. "You don't have to be like an Oreo cookie, brother," as Ballard put it. After one particularly frank network appearance, Brown had been investigated (and then exonerated) by the Federal Communications Commission for voicing his opinion about the various strains of African-Americans. "A colored man is a man afraid to stand up and face his own convictions," Brown suggested, while a Negro is someone "who doesn't want to be identified with the ghetto." Brown, says Sharpton, was always quick to determine the relative "blackness" of the leaders and fellow entertainers he met. According to Sharpton, Brown once interrupted a famous black leader during a conversation in Las Vegas to point out the difference between the leader and Rev. Sharpton. *"He's* a James Brown man," he said, pointing to the minister. "He's raw. You're . . . *acceptable.* Which is all right, but it ain't raw. It ain't hard enough."

Ballard's other political recording bore the unlikely title "How You Gonna Get Respect (When You Haven't Cut Your Process Yet)." In mid-1968, James Brown cut his hair. In black and white America alike, hairstyles were, of course, fashion polemics at the time. *HAIR: The American Tribal Love-Rock Musical* became the talk of Broadway when it opened in April. While the white children of the Age of Aquarius were making statements with their gender-bending hairstyles, black Americans were denouncing the so-called "process," the painstaking procedure of having one's hair straightened by "cooking" it with lye.

Malcolm X made the process—the "conk"—a metaphoric reminder of his early days as a hustler on the streets of Roxbury in *The Autobiography of Malcolm X,* published the year of his death, 1965. "A can of Red Devil lye, two eggs, and two medium-sized white potatoes" made up the shopping list for his first conk, as he recalled. Though he gladly suffered the pain of the process ("the comb felt as if it was raking my skin off"), he later came to see a black man's conk as "the emblem of his shame that he is black." "This was my first really big step toward self-degradation: when I endured all of that pain, literally burning my flesh to have it look like a white man's hair," he wrote. To the mature Malcolm, conking, and the wigs worn by black women, were "ridiculous" efforts to deny their natural blackness. "It makes you wonder if the Negro has completely lost his sense of identity," he lamented.

Other black leaders seconded the notion. "We have to stop being ashamed of being black," said Stokely Carmichael. "A broad nose, a thick lip, and nappy hair is us and we are going to call that beautiful whether they like it or not. We are not going to fry our hair anymore." By 1968 Malcolm's message about the symbolic importance of going "natural"—cultivating, rather than ironing out, the tight kinks of black hair—was a widely accepted gesture of the cultural revolution. Sidney Poitier and Muhammad Ali wore naturals. The Panthers wore naturals; the Nation wore naturals.

But James Brown had come of age in the 1940s and '50s, when conking was a badge of hipness. All of his inspirations, from Ellington, Cab Calloway, and Louis Jordan to Little Richard, had worn some form of relaxer-aided hairstyle, and Brown's own image was based in part on the ever-changing contours of his luxurious pompadour. "The man spent more time in curlers than Edna Turnblad in *Hairspray*," joked the writer Gerri Hirshey, a longtime confidante of Brown's, in the obituary she wrote for *Rolling Stone*. Henry Stallings, a close friend of the singer from their school days together, traveled for much of his life with the entertainer in a dual role—bodyguard and hairstylist.

In the thick of the culture wars of the 1960s, however, Brown somewhat reluctantly renounced his process. "It was like givin' up something for Lent," as he later said. "I wanted people to know that one of the most prized things I let go of was my hair. It was a real attraction to my business. But I would cut it off for the movement."

Ballard, like Brown, was from the old school, but he too was ready to make a fashion statement in the name of black pride. "So get that mess out of your hair, and wear your natural 'do/ And I'm gonna bet on my dear life, respect gonna come to you," he sang. They almost certainly weren't his own words alone. After the recording of "Say It Loud—I'm Black and I'm Proud" in July, Brown insisted that the entire entourage switch to short Afros like his. Brown would retain the look for a handful of years before returning to the beauty parlor in the mid-1970s.

Brown's Afros, needless to say, were painstakingly teased, sometimes close to the scalp, sometimes, as on the cover of the 1971 Live-at-the-Apollo-III release *Revolution of the Mind*, the size and lopsided shape of a partially deflated basketball. To the singer, the look was just another example of righteousness. "He was so minute with the uniforms, all the bow ties had to be the same width," said Maceo Parker in a 1997 interview. "He preached pride, dignity, you've got to watch what you say, what you're doing about the ladies."

In the same interview, Parker expressed his belief in separating show business from politics. "I don't want to get too left, too right, too front, too back," he said. "To me, entertainers don't really belong in that kind of thing. I don't really want to be known as a Republican, I don't want to be known as a Democrat. . . . I associate funky music with the partying mood—'Now we're going to lay our political beliefs outside for a minute, and we're just going to party.'" He certainly needed to call on that conviction to get through his comedy routine on the night after King's assassination.

After Whitney left the stage at the Garden, Parker made an announcement. Reports were, he said, that the city was quiet, and that the broadcast was successfully keeping people at home. "I think the fact that we do have the television cameras here, I think it was a big success," he said. "Thank you very kindly." Then he took the opportunity to insert a plug for the souvenir programs available in the lobby.

Inside the arena, it was business as usual for James Brown and his band. Outside, however, the city was a ghost town. Parker was handed a note, from which he announced some garbled train-and-bus updates. "The only transportation out of Dudley Street Station is to Allston," he said. "For transportation to Dorchester, go to Eggleston Square. Y'understand?" None of this meant anything to the North Carolina native, who fumbled through the pronunciation of the place names. To the audience, however, the message was clear: The city was actively discouraging travel both into and out of its black neighborhoods.

Parker was more familiar with his next bit of duty, the one commonly associated with longtime Brown emcee Danny Ray. "Right now, ladies and gentlemen, it's showtime!" the young saxophonist rumbled. (Ray would amend the introduction to "Star Time!") "Introducing the young man that you chose to be Soul Brother Number One." Then began the famous list of song titles, each followed by a one-note exclamation point banged out in unison by trumpet, guitar, and drum. "The man who sings 'Try Me' "—bam—" 'Prisoner of Love' "—bam, a half-step higher—" 'Papa's Got a Brand New Bag' "—another half-step—"I break out in a 'Cold Sweat' . . . 'Get It Together' . . . 'I Can't Stand Myself' . . . 'There Was a Time' . . . his very latest release, 'I Got the Feelin'' . . . I've got the feelin'! Here he is, along with the world's [sic] Famous Flames, Mr. Please Please Please himself . . . JAMES BROWN!" The fanfare as Brown ascended the stairs from beneath the stage was designed to inspire pandemonium, with the trumpeters and Jimmy Nolen trading frantic blows from their respective instruments, as if the last round were ticking down.

"Oo *wee!*" Brown yipped as he lunged for the microphone. "Done got wise!" The song was "Get It Together," the lengthy (nearly nine minutes in the unedited original) two-part single released in October. As insistent as the recorded version was, in performance it was a crackling live wire, a funky tour de force that throbbed with a rowdy, almost psychedelic go-go vibe. Like so many of Brown's songs, "Get It Together" could be heard on multiple levels—as a kiss-off to a wayward lover, or a challenge to underachievers. Whoever he's addressing dropped out of school "before you got it down," he charged. And that, he said, alluding as he so often did to his own disappointing lack of education, "ain't hip."

He acknowledged "the lovely Miss Ann Norman," by then the sole dancer touring with the Revue, who was shimmying in knee-high boots and a micro-miniskirt on a riser behind the drum kit. As the band crashed ahead with wave upon wave of the song's six-note motif, the singer implored his guitarist to "give me a little Wes Montgomery right about now." Nolen obliged with several bars of finger-plucked octaves, emulating the bop guitarist's "Naptown sound," named for Indianapolis, Montgomery's hometown.

Following solos for Parker and baritone saxophonist St. Clair Pinckney, the band suddenly kicked into the locomotive rhythm machine of "There Was a Time." After the speeches, the ballads, the featured vocalists, and the comedy routine, this was the part of the show that would grasp for real transcendence.

"The one thing that can solve most of our problems is dancing," Brown once said, and he was suddenly determined to prove the point. "There Was a Time," a staple of the live show released as the B-side of "I Can't Stand Myself" in December, was a hard-funk update of one of Brown's old tropes, a call list of popular dance moves that he could demonstrate. The showcase invariably pushed his audience toward euphoria: the Mashed Potatoes, a kind of one-legged Twist; the Jerk, a hip-thrusting move that had been called lewd a decade earlier; the Camel Walk, a bow-legged, hunched-shoulder strut; the Boogaloo, a Latin-style body roll performed with one hand raised overhead. The crowd in Boston knew what was next, and the singer let them show it. "You can bet, haven't seen nothin' yet, until you see me do the—WHAT?" he asked. "The James Brown!" the small throng boomed back.

Brown's signature dance was, in fact, whatever he wanted it to be. As an admiring writer for *Dance* magazine explained many years later, it was a synthesis of seemingly every dance craze to hit the ballrooms since the Lindy Hop—"an indescribably fast and furious combination of the slide, slop, funky chicken, mashed potato, camel walk, shimmy, applejack, and quiver." The cleansing power of dance later became, in Brown's world, the "good foot," as coined on his 1972 single "Get on the Good Foot." Just as "Funky Drummer" was the groove that launched a thousand raps, hip-hop historians often maintain that the "Good Foot" concept marked the creation of b-boy breakdance culture. For all the brashness of Brown's vocalization—"I like being loud and letting people know I'm there," he once said—his sensational presence was always equally marked by the vitality expressed in his nonstop movement.

He epitomized the life force. "People who truly dance are those who have never bartered the fierce freedom of their souls," wrote the Trinidadian immigrant Pearl Primus, the renowned social-protest dancer, choreographer, and anthropologist. Belief, Primus argued, is essential to dance; "dance without belief, though often very well done, is without life." For Brown to dance with such determination one night after King's murder meant that life would, in fact, go on for the living.

"You got that feeling?" Brown asked, moving to the music like a stunt pilot in high winds. "Everybody over there got that feelin'?" ("Yeah!") "Then stand up and be counted. *Good Gawd.*"

He could have counted them himself. The small gathering was there at the Garden, as much as the singer was, to prove the point—the show must go on. As it was nationally, the black minority in Boston was growing, but in relative terms. Though rising dramatically, the number of African-Americans in Boston still represented less than 20 percent of the population. And while black America would account for twenty-two million residents in 1970, according to the U.S. Census Bureau—more than twice as many African-Americans as there had been fifty years earlier—that figure remained 11 percent of all Americans. If the civil rights movement relied on numbers—registering voters, reducing unemployment, banding together to break down barriers—for Brown, the best measure of black pride was his own career. To him, each new million-selling record signified a million more Americans with *soul*, that intangible characteristic that meant dauntlessness if it meant anything.

"Try me," Brown abruptly crooned, reining in the mayhem he was causing with two bending, beseeching syllables. Even during a song crafted to be so atypically vulnerable—"And your love will stop my heart from dying"—he exuded dash and certitude. As Parker and Pinckney stepped into the spotlight, framing the singer with their dueling tenor saxophones, mirroring each other with a few elegant front-and-back steps in gleaming patent leather shoes as they puffed the song's dreamy instrumental bridge, Brown worked out, incongruously, as if training with an imaginary jump rope. He pivoted, snapped his fingers, hollered off-microphone; he jerked his right elbow on cue with one of Stubblefield's out-of-nowhere snare hits. Then, after a brief placekeeping interlude, the band rumbled into the hypnotic bustle of "Cold Sweat."

"I don't care! About your past," Brown sang, living, as ever, precisely in the moment. After the song came around to the "So What" motif for the second time, he casually alluded to a few other numbers that had had the audacity to vie with his own on the charts. "Love me do. Funky, funky Broadway," Brown warbled, in one absentminded ad-lib challenging both the sustained supremacy of the Beatles and the more immediate threat of the short-lived Buffalo soul group Dyke and the Blazers, whose "Funky Broadway" had inspired a Wilson Pickett cover version that had been a massive R&B hit the previous summer.

As the bandleader lost himself in his orchestra's metronomic black magic, first Parker, then Stubblefield took extended solos. Snapping to, Brown grunted along with Stubblefield's emphatic cymbal crashes—"ooh ooh, ah, ooh, ah!"—before turning to the crowd. "I want everybody to put your hands together and give me some of that *olllld* soul," he shouted, squealing the last two words as the band slipped into a fragment of "Ride Your Pony," a 1965 hit by the funky New Orleanian Lee Dorsey. Produced by Allen Toussaint with musical accompaniment by the very young Crescent City musicians who would become the Meters, Dorsey's "Ride Your Pony" was a shout-out to whistle-stops across the country—New York, Detroit, Atlanta G-A, *Californ-eye-ay*—along the order of Brown's own version of "Night Train." With the mode of transportation a cowboy's bronco rather than a Pullman sleeper, the song celebrated the Wild West. "Now shoot, shoot, shoot," clucked Dorsey, a smooth-faced former boxer, on the original recording. Each command had been followed by the sound of a gunshot.

"Everybody got the feelin'?" Brown asked, as the band stripped down to Stubblefield's heavy shuffle and Drummond's undulating bass, with Nolen's repeating three-note cluster acting as a buoy, bobbing up on the other side of each rhythmic wave. *"Does everybody got the feelin'?"*

Suddenly, one young man is overcome. Oh, yes, he has the feeling. In a black leather car coat and a close-cropped Afro, he emerges from a thicket of raised hands, vaulting onstage at Brown's feet. Instantly he is pushed back down by one, and then two men in suits, who hustle from the shadows at either side of the stage. On bass, Drummond almost imperceptibly flubs a note, as if to mutter an "Uh-oh" under his breath. As Brown gets the crowd to count the bars to the next clamorous reintroduction of the full band, another man—the same?—tries again, and then another time, to mount the stage. Each time he is greeted with a rude shove.

What does he want? Surely, just to dance for a moment with his idol. But this is a season of paranoia. The shots that rocked the sixties have put an entire nation on high alert. In thousands of homes and apartments across the greater Boston area, viewers hoping to drown out the terrible truth of King's murder sit up in their easy chairs.

Onstage, the band plunges back into "Cold Sweat." Brown whips his neck to one side, butting heads with the beat. Big drops of perspiration fly off his forehead in the light. It's as though he is illustrating the lyric. His hair has become a thatch of unmoored wool. Brown calls off the band, then leads them into a punchy version of "Maybe the Last Time," the song he released coincidentally with the dismissal of the Famous Flames in 1964.

The stage, already chaotic with musicians, backup singers, and entourage members pressed into service as bodyguards, grows ominously more crowded as two robust Boston police officers in full regalia step to the lip, pointing into the throng, then crouching. As if on cue, the scene cuts to the reverse camera, situated behind the stage, as it zooms in on a section of the audience, seen conspicuously for the first time all evening. Several fans are swaying, clapping; a woman in a sweater and an oversized necklace swivels her hips and tosses a fist to the snare drum. But many more seem taken aback. They crane toward the stage, wondering what to make of this sudden prospect of confrontation. A young man in a flat newsboy cap stands sideways, one shoulder pointing toward the singer, motionless. "Maybe the LA-AST TIME!" Brown howls. "Oh I, oh I, *don't know.*"

The singer, still smiling, starts a new chant, asking his audience to "shake hands with your best friend." He reaches down and begins clasping outstretched hands, which quickly multiply into a tangle. Like a candidate facing a narrow deficit on election eve, he makes his way toward stage right, leaning into the crowd as he attempts to make contact with each extended palm. The gesture immediately attracts a phalanx of security. Members of Brown's entourage and the police force surround the singer, shuffling together in a slow-motion scrum across the edge of the stage. One teenaged black boy in a white-on-white outfit pulls himself up to sit on the stage, grinning broadly and waving toward the audience. Eventually he is coaxed down.

There are now more than a half-dozen officers onstage; one of them, surprisingly for Boston in 1968, is a black man. Their brass buttons reflect the spotlight. The singer steps back from his fans and blows kisses toward the rafters. On the riser behind the drum kit, Ann Norman's white fringe swirls. Brown rejoins the microphone, and the camera meets him there; for a moment the authorities are out of sight. Hands reach toward his knees; something—a pen?—flies through the air and lands near his feet. "I feel all right!" he brays. On the broadcast, a flash washes out the image.

★ ★ ★ 9 ★ ★ ★

GET IT TOGETHER

"**P**lease Please Please" was, on this night, no kind of plea—it was an order. The cape went on; the cape came off. He was too exhausted to continue; he had to continue. James Brown's determination to carry out the burlesque of his cape routine had never been more obvious, and it nearly caused the riot the city of Boston was striving to contain.

As a child in South Carolina, he had worn stitched panels from flour sacks. Struggling to make it as far as the seventh grade at Augusta's segregated Silas X. Floyd School, his wardrobe consisted of tattered overalls. He was routinely dismissed from class on charges of "insufficient clothes." "It made me feel terrible," he would recall, "and I never forgot it."

It's easy to see how that kind of humiliation would have compelled the grown man's adamant insistence on maintaining a meticulous wardrobe. In the early years of his career it was the satin tuxedos of the doo-wop era—suits that started out in black and white before blooming into vivid Technicolor, like the movies. The trim, cosmopolitan lines of his suits of the late 1960s gradually gave way to some outrageous, glittering bodysuits and superhero-style costumes in the following decade. When Brown's long career finally began to flag, he gravitated toward Napoleonic military jackets in electric hues. Ratifying the spit-shined rigor for which his bands were often noted, James Brown called his last touring band the Soul Generals.

For Brown, the clothes were a critical part of the show, and any public appearance, however fleeting, was showtime. (This is why the lurid mugshots taken after his late-life arrests—unruly tumbleweeds of hair, gray chin stubble—have retained such seamy effect: They are entirely at odds with the man's fastidiously cultivated persona.) The legendary fines he laid on members of his band were typically administered for grooming infractions. In the 1960s he docked his salaried musicians $25 for scuffed shoes, twice that for unpressed suits.

The legendary cape, the key prop at virtually every show he ever did, was, with its sequins, rich velour, and glittering "God-father of Soul" emblem, the splashy regalia of self-proclaimed royalty. Brown often credited Gorgeous George, the primping, preening wrestler in sequined robes who answered to the nick-name the Human Orchid, as an inspiration. To Brown, like his friend Muhammad Ali, who also acknowledged a debt to Gorgeous George, self-promotion was by nature shameless.

The novelist Jonathan Lethem, in a *Rolling Stone* cover profile published a few months before Brown's death, wondered whether the cape act might have represented not just the singer's princely self-image, but also, in the casting off, a secret desire to expose his own private shortcomings. It was, Lethem proposed, "a rehearsal onstage of the succor James Brown could never accept in his real life. It is as though, having come from being dressed in potato sacks for grade school and in the drab uniform of a prisoner to being the most spectacularly garbed individual this side of Beau Brummell or Liberace, James Brown found himself compelled also to be the Emperor With No Clothes."

After the cape act and the nearly disastrous storming of the stage, the Garden concert ended hastily, in another "Cold Sweat." As Brown stalked the boards ghosted by a flashing strobe effect, one of the trumpets squealed at the upper reaches of the band's fevered exit music. After twenty-four hours of psychic distress over the King assassination, and two hours and fourteen minutes of high-strung performance under heavy police protection and the unforgiving interrogation of the television cameras, James Brown and his barnstorming orchestra were mercifully finished for the night.

Their usefulness, however, had not yet expired. The broadcast would be repeated immediately, in an effort to keep people safely in their living rooms. When the first ninety-minute reel ran out, one of the WGBH staff members had driven it across town to the station on Western Avenue in the Allston neighborhood, across the Charles River from Harvard Square. On television, Bill Pierce, the very proper elocutionist who was the longtime voice of WGBH, made an announcement.

"In just a moment we're going to do something rather wild for television," he said, sounding, in his honeyed sonority, anything but wild. "We're going to repeat tonight's concert—James Brown and his troupe." (Two hours earlier, he'd introduced the program by "the Negro singer Jimmy Brown.") After thanking the American Federation of Television and Radio Artists and the American Federation of Musicians, Pierce noted that there were surely James Brown fans in Boston who were unaware of the telecast. "If you have any friends who would've enjoyed tonight's concert at the Boston Garden, won't you tell them that we're going to repeat the show right now?" he suggested pleasantly. Kevin White might have given the appeal a bit more urgency.

Dana Chandler was at home on Moreland Street with his wife and children, watching the concert. The artist had spent the day attending protest meetings and attempting to mediate between the police and agitated youths on the streets outside Roxbury's Orchard Park housing project. "As much as these kids were claiming they were having a bad time over Martin Luther King," he recalls, "they were having a good time at the thought of being able to throw some stones at some cops. Because at that time, of course, if you were a young black person, you had already been harassed. I can remember in the fifties the number of times I was stopped by a police officer just walking home at night. And it hadn't changed much at all by the time '68 came around, when I was twenty-seven. . . . It was a very tough time to be young and black in Boston."

To Chandler, Brown's impact on this day was a logical extension of the image the singer had created for himself. When the threat of violence flared, the singer's command of both the police and the crowd was a dramatic act by a man accustomed to taking charge. James Brown, says Chandler, "was a *man*. And he never allowed them to see him as anything less. It was like having a father or your uncle—or your African elder, for that matter—walk out in the middle of the stage and tell [the young people] that they were not doing themselves or the community any service by acting fool up on that stage."

"James Brown, the noted rock 'n' roll performer, usually breeds anything but tranquility," as a *Wall Street Journal* editorial head-lined NONVIOLENT ROCK noted a few days after the show. "Deliri-ous crowds go into a frenzy when his gyrating hips take off in a wild bugaloo [sic] or other popular dance, and they respond vociferously to his screaming songs." Brown, the paper went on to propose, "might seem an unlikely apostle of Martin Luther King's message of nonviolence. But one could hardly have found a more effective one last Friday night."

Brown, ever impervious, would claim that he never felt undue pressure from the spotlight in Boston. "People still ask me if I was frightened that night, and of course the answer is, I wasn't," as he put it in his 2005 memoir. (Years later, a Cambridge plan-ning consultant who had attended the show with his wife met Kevin White at a reception. When the man recalled how ap-prehensive he had been, the mayor replied, "Not anywhere near as frightened as I was.") The young people who vaulted onstage were, Brown felt, no threat: "They wanted an explanation, a reason why, not more violence."

But Marva Whitney, who was perhaps closer to the singer than anyone at the time (he asked her to marry him, she says, though she declined), believes the whole episode took something out of Brown. "I know he went through something mentally," she says. "He knew whether it went down wrong, bad, indiffer-ent, whatever, he knew that he would get blamed for it. To tell you the truth, I was glad when we got out of there."

What was "truly scary," as *Newsweek*'s David Gates, who at-tended the show, would reminisce almost forty years later, following Brown's death, "was how he made a crucial moment in American history vanish for two hours by pulling us into private worlds of passion, pleasure, pain, and joy. . . . He could have torn the city apart. All he did was tear me apart, along with everybody else."

Across the country, cities were in fact coming unglued. In Chicago, hundreds of families were left homeless as large sections of the West Side burned; six men, all black, were dead in shooting incidents. The riots in Baltimore, which did not begin until Saturday, eventually would result in six deaths, seven hundred injuries, more than four thousand arrests, and more than a thousand reported arson cases. That city featured reports of Rap Brown driving around in a Ford Mustang, exhorting protesters. (King's murderer, James Earl Ray, was also said to be driving a Mustang.) Baltimore also had the spectacle of Maryland Governor Spiro Agnew calling in massive National Guard and state police presence, then laying the blame for the rioting at the feet of the city's black leadership. "I call on you to publicly repudiate all black racists," Agnew roared in a staged confrontation. His attention-grabbing ploy raised his national profile to such an extent that he would soon be chosen as Richard Nixon's running mate.

In New York, Police Commissioner Howard Leary lamented that the vandals seemed so young. "Sixty percent of the looters were under sixteen," he claimed: "What are we supposed to do, shoot the next Martin Luther King?" Thousands marched on City Hall in protest. James Forman, the former SNCC president, recognized "the end of tactical non-violence" and called for "instant retribution" at a rally in Central Park. "We have to die destroying this country to build a better one," he said, advocating the destruction of power stations and "making some of these big tall buildings tumble." (On Long Island, seven-year-old Carlton Ridenhour, who would grow up to be Public Enemy's Chuck D, experienced the chaos as "a mass of debris, almost like the World Trade Center collapsing.") With well over one hundred cities across the nation reporting incidents ranging from bottle-throwing and window-smashing to assault, arson, and point-blank murder, the damage total eventually would be set at $45 million: at least thirty-nine deaths, well over three thousand injured, tens of thousands more arrested. Detroit, Memphis, Nashville, and Washington, D.C., were among the cities to declare curfews. Meanwhile, in Plains, Georgia, Rosalynn Carter, the future First Lady, noted sadly that a local bar was giving away free beer to celebrate the assassination. International observers were appalled by the whole spectacle. The riots were "the disintegration of everything that makes up the life of a civilized collectivity," declared Le Monde.

Washington was hardest hit. More than twelve thousand troops were ordered into the city as broad sections of the downtown area raged in flames. Just south of the intersection of 14th and U Streets, near Sam's Pawnbrokers and the Rhodes Five and Ten, Stokely Carmichael confronted rioters on the city streets, grabbing a gun from one man's hands. When a protester argued that the black community had lost its leader, Carmichael responded, "You won't get one like this! You'll just get shot." Frightened businesspeople and government workers, unable to find transportation out of the gridlocked city, crossed the Memorial Bridge over the Potomac River on foot. Five residents were dead by Saturday morning, nearly one thousand arrested. Clark Clifford, the country's Secretary of Defense, later noted that, just two months after the beginning of the Tet Offensive in South Vietnam, "it seemed as if we were experiencing our own national uprising. As I drove from my house to the Pentagon the morning after Dr. King's death, I could see the smoke rising from the inner city, only ten blocks from the White House."

Mayor Walter Washington declared a moratorium on the sale of gasoline and alcohol. He had been appointed to his post in 1967 by President Johnson after declining it the previous year, when he had not been granted commission over the police and fire departments. Although FBI Director J. Edgar Hoover reportedly urged Washington to command the troops to shoot to kill, the mayor rejected it. Instead, he too took to the streets, personally asking looters and rioters to turn back.

The mayor contacted Dewey Hughes, the news director at WOL, an AM radio station ("Where Information Is Power") that was the city's top-rated R&B outlet. Hughes, in turn, contacted Brown's entourage, and the singer agreed to help. "By that time I had received several requests like that from different cities," Brown would claim, "but I went to Washington because it was really the symbol of the whole country." Brown took the jet to the nation's capital and went on local television station WTTG, making a live address in the early afternoon from the Municipal Center. "I know how everybody feels," he said. "I feel the same way. But you can't accomplish anything by blowing up, burning up, stealing, and looting. Don't terrorize. Organize. Don't burn. Give kids a chance to learn. . . . The real answer to race problems in this country is education. Be ready. Be qualified. Own something. Be somebody. That's black power." He dreamed, he said, of achieving an "upper level for my people . . . I want you to be presidents and things." He went on the air at WOL and made the same appeal. While he was in the city, Lady Bird Johnson and the president and First Lady's daughter, Luci Nugent, both called to extend their gratitude. "I think that was an audience the station didn't usually get," Brown joked.

"He accomplished his mission somewhat," says Marva Whitney of Brown's effort in the capital. "They still tore the mother up, but it could've been worse." But the singer, who had praised the United States as "the greatest country in the world"—"We've come too far to throw it away," he reportedly said—also took a heavy dose of criticism. Many Washingtonians were openly hostile toward the singer, recalls Kenny Hull, who was first hired as a roadie in 1961 after befriending the group during Brown's regular Howard Theatre appearances in D.C. He had been entrusted with the singer's personal well-being since one particularly disorderly show in the early 1960s. When local police left the band members to fend for themselves, Brown had some trouble getting off the stage. Hull, acting like a blocking fullback, lowered his shoulders and cleared a path for the singer. "From then on, he said, 'You're with me.' "

As the rioting in Washington continued, disgruntled fans shouted down the singer, calling him "Sold Brother Number One." Some demanded to know why he still straightened his hair. Fearing for the boss's safety, Hull practically had to drag Brown out of the city. "You didn't argue with him," he says, "but I kind of got a little hostile with him. Shit, I was scared there myself."

From the chaotic Washington visit Brown reunited that evening with the band in Rochester, New York, their next scheduled tour stop, at the War Memorial Auditorium. Four years earlier Rochester had suffered through a race riot that had crippled the city's self-image. Once called "Smugtown" for the economic security engendered by the presence of such industry giants as Eastman Kodak, the city witnessed four deaths, more than three hundred reported injuries, and eight hundred arrests during the 1964 strife, which began over the allegedly abusive arrest of a drunk-and-disorderly African-American man at a block party. Now, as the disturbances in the aftermath of King's murder continued into the weekend, Mayor Frank Lamb asked the visiting soul singer for his help. Brown's call for calm in Rochester earned him a proclamation from the mayor and a thank-you from the chief of police, who called the singer's assistance "a major contribution to maintaining peace and tranquility in our community."

Back in Boston, the situation was contained, though not entirely peaceful. Despite the fact that the city was widely noted for keeping cool, incidents of looting and vandalism persisted for several days. Sections of Blue Hill Avenue, the busy thoroughfare that runs through Roxbury and Dorchester, were burning, and there was considerable damage. "I remember kids were carrying out TV sets" from smashed storefronts, recalls Paul Parks. Looters lined up the contents of a shoe store out on the sidewalk, so that residents could have their pick of the bounty. The city operated under emergency conditions through the weekend. Several cultural events were canceled, including a Pearl Bailey concert at the Back Bay Theater and weekend performances of *You're a Good Man, Charlie Brown.* By Sunday, twenty-one injuries, "about thirty" arrests, and four multiple-alarm fires had been reported.

In the end, however, the streets of Boston were undoubtedly less volatile than they might have been.

Tom Atkins, the councilor, was having a taxing weekend. "The mayor was lauded in the national media for this stroke of brilliance," as the councilor would tell Henry Hampton. "I, on the other hand, got sick." On Saturday, he was treated for a high fever at the Harvard infirmary. "On Monday morning I got a call from James Brown. He'd been told the city was going to back out of its agreement to guarantee the gate. I had a hundred-and-three fever, but I felt an obligation to Mr. Brown." In an afternoon meeting with the mayor, a feverish Atkins threatened to "publicize it in the council" if the city tried to shirk its responsibility.

By all indications, the entertainer eventually got paid. Exactly how much, no one seems to know. According to some reports the Vault contributed $15,000. By Tuesday, another $2,150 had been raised through a special Martin Luther King, Jr., fund at City Hall.

As Atkins had been quoted in the Sunday *Globe*, James Brown deserved a "tremendous vote of thanks." He'd demonstrated "how to talk to young people in a language they both understood and accepted. His kind of message goes beyond the realm of black or white—it is universal." The show, the *Harvard Crimson* editorialized in its Monday edition, "was an unbelievable demonstration of how a man like James Brown coupled with mass media could be used for political purposes." (Not that the writer was a fan, exactly: "The thought of politicians turning to rock groups for popular support is a bit frightening.") On Thursday, the eleventh, a front-page story in the weekly *Bay State Banner*, headlined JAMES BROWN HELPS OUT, excerpted a letter submitted by an unidentified Roxbury woman. "If the James Brown show had not been televised," she wrote, "Roxbury probably would have been in shambles Saturday morning."

WGBH ran the show twice more over the weekend, and the mayor was effusive in his praise for the station. "Your immediate willingness to televise the Brown show, and the speed and efficiency with which you carried this out on such short notice, contributed as much as any other event to the atmosphere of conciliation which prevailed in Boston this past week," he wrote.

To Chuck Turner, the Black United Front organizer who would eventually become a city councilor himself, Brown, the White administration, and the television station certainly deserved credit. However, he would recall years later on WGBH's long-running African-American affairs program *Say Brother* (which debuted in July 1968—a direct result of the station's increased commitment to black viewers in the aftermath of the concert broadcast), the emphasis on their roles overshadowed the critical commitment of community leaders whose own diligence helped keep the peace. Lt. Gov. Francis W. Sargent, who would become the state's next governor, was among those who did recognize those efforts. "While other American cities were in flames," he said, "our people have reacted with dignity and restraint to the death of Martin Luther King. . . . This was particularly true of the leadership in Roxbury. They did more than the government did."

The urge toward accountability had been widespread. Representatives of the Urban League and Operation Exodus distributed "survival sheets" with emergency contact numbers. An operation called the New England Grass Roots Organization—NEGRO—served as a communications center, with a street patrol reporting disturbances by walkie-talkie and citizens' band radio. On WILD, disc jockeys kept up a running stream of updates, interspersed with memorial services for King and call-in opportunities for residents in need of emotional venting. One group, the Roxbury Youth Alliance, had developed out of the Freedom Security Patrol formed to accompany Dr. King on his last visit to Boston, in 1965, when he had marched in the rain with thousands of supporters to the Boston Common. In a cruel irony, King's assassination compelled the Youth Alliance to resurrect its dormant Security Patrol to monitor the streets.

Chief among the community's concerns was to minimize contact with the Boston police department—to prove that black Boston could police its own. "Everybody in the black community cooperated with one another," Al Thomas, identified as a father of six, told the *Banner.* "We showed that black people can take care of black people." The police department soon retreated. "I don't know what happened to The Man," said twenty-four-year-old Ossie Jordan, who was working the phones at the Roxbury YMCA. "Maybe they were just told to lighten up." Others credited the force for its restraint: "I think there's been one thousand percent improvement by police over last year," said Joseph Gupton, an official for Attack Committee, a Blue Hill Avenue neighborhood association, referring to the rioting triggered the previous June by the welfare sit-in at Grove Hall.

While neighborhood leaders such as Bryant Rollins, Rev. Virgil Wood, Leroy Boston, and Mel King (who would go on to run a strong mayoral campaign against Kevin White's eventual successor, Ray Flynn, in 1983) quickly took it upon themselves to calm the community, they also seized the opportunity to mount an unprecedented protest against unfavorable conditions for blacks in Boston. "We started talking to the young people," said YMCA director Bill Wimberly, "and we did not tell them what to do . . . We counseled them on bail procedures if they got arrested, if that way was going to be their choice." One of Wimberly's associates wore a button on his raincoat above his armband. The button read, AMERICA IS THE BLACK MAN'S BATTLE GROUND.

While the grief was palpable, so too was the feeling that this could finally mark the chance for black Bostonians to be heard. "People didn't go home, didn't eat," recalled Leroy Boston, later known as Alajo Adegballoh. "*Law* was made there." He came out of the crisis deeply encouraged by his community's invigorated sense of purpose and commitment: "That short period of time we were the people's government," he said. "Roxbury was unto itself." By Saturday evening, the police department could announce that it had reverted to "normal" patrols across the city.

"I am proud of my people for not resorting to the streets," wrote Judith Edwards, a Roxbury resident, in a letter published in the *Banner* on Thursday. "I know there were some outbreaks, but I think had it not been for James Brown, things would have been much worse." Brown, she wrote, "holds a place in my heart": "This man has black power and know[s] how to use it." Dr. King, she concluded, "would have been proud if he could have seen how the people of Boston, his second home, upheld his beliefs."

On Saturday, the sixth, the Rev. Michael E. Haynes, Dr. King's onetime associate at the Twelfth Baptist Church in Roxbury, led a memorial service for the slain leader. Among those in attendance were Mayor White, Lt. Gov. Sargent, and McNamara, the police commissioner. When White returned that afternoon to City Hall, he encountered a group of two hundred protesters, mostly white college students, representing the New England Draft Resistance and another group known as People

Against Racism. NO COPS IN THE GHETTO, read one of their signs. The Resistance was promoting a general strike among students and faculty in the Boston area during the upcoming week, to demand an end to racism and the Vietnam War.

On Monday two distinct events took place. An estimated thirty thousand people, many of them members of the white middle class, attended a memorial service on the Boston Common, with addresses by Mayor White, Lt. Gov. Sargent, Cardinal Cushing—the Archbishop of Boston and a member of the NAACP—and others. Meanwhile, another assembly took place a few miles away in Franklin Park, the five-hundred-acre woodland bordering the Roxbury and Jamaica Plain neighborhoods designed by Frederick Law Olmsted. At Franklin Park, thousands gathered inside White Stadium for a rally at which the Black United Front's twenty-one demands were declared. Overhead flew the Black Nationalist flag of Marcus Garvey. "We took down the flag which has dishonored us," said Rev. Virgil Wood, as he invited the gathering to sing not "the anthem that has dishonored us, but the one that has honored us"—James Weldon Johnson's "Lift Every Voice and Sing."

A contingent from the White Stadium rally also ventured downtown to join the memorial service on the Common, where they requested speaking time. The well-meaning liberals, says Bryant Rollins, were taken aback by the group's declaration of black solidarity. "I'll never forget it," Rollins says. "We said, 'We cannot rely on this system to take care of us. We need to get ourselves together.' It was quite dramatic. We were at this rally created by people saying we need to live and work together. But the black folks were saying, 'We need to pull out.' The folks who organized it were really upset."

Kevin White felt emboldened when, in mid-April, he went to the members of the Vault to ask for help in paying James Brown. He took the opportunity to ask for an additional million dollars to offer Boston's black community, to be earmarked for development opportunities. The boardroom veterans of the Vault—among them the presidents of the First National Bank of Boston and Gillette and executives of the Liberty Mutual Insurance Company, the New England Merchants Bank, and the department stores Filene's and Jordan Marsh—were ill-prepared for that kind of demand. "Well, gentlemen, the city is at stake here, so whatever you think you can do," White reportedly said. Within a half hour, White, back in his office, was informed that he had been granted $100,000. Paying Brown had been a sticking point, as Vault treasurer Ephron Catlin later attested, but the mayor had convinced them "the blacks were going to burn the city down" if the guarantee for the singer wasn't produced. The cost of covering the singer's fee, as the mayor suggested, was potentially cheaper than the costs that would have been incurred by rebuilding if a real riot had broken out downtown.

Vault funds, administered on the mayor's behalf by Barney Frank, were eventually parceled out for such programs as Roxbury Beautification and tickets for underprivileged children to attend the Ice Capades at the Garden. Meanwhile, a businessman named Sheldon Appel was moved by Bill Wimberly's plea in the *Herald-Traveler* article for a badly needed new gym for the kids of Roxbury, which, said the YMCA director, would cost $250,000. Appel approached Ralph Hoagland, president of the CVS drugstore chain, who had taught business classes in Roxbury. Hoagland was friendly with Bryant Rollins, who brought his attention to the Black United Front's unprecedented demand at the rally in Franklin Park—$100 million in development money, without stipulations. Mayor White was indignant. "Social reform rarely benefits from expropriation," he complained, refusing to negotiate with the Front.

Undaunted, Hoagland and Appel took it upon themselves to try to raise the hundred million, organizing a series of breakfast meetings with other suburban-based business executives and asking each for a thousand-dollar pledge. In late May the Fund for United Negro Development (FUND) delivered its first check of $75,000 to a contingent from the Black United Front at the Somerset Hotel. "The self-interest in such a project for Boston businessmen was evident—they didn't want to be treated to a Detroit-like riot," Mel King would write. "But FUND was a milestone in terms of freeing money for Black development that was not to be shaped by the will of the white donors." Kevin White, however, led the charge of skepticism about the Black United Front. Hoagland's colleagues had picked "the wrong black cats," he argued. "If they go out and buy machine guns, I'm holding you people personally responsible for the bloodbath."

Ultimately, FUND would provide a million dollars through 1972, mostly in the form of small-business loans. Meanwhile, White's official alternative, the Boston Urban Foundation (BUF), took the same acronym as the Black United Front. Supported by the brotherhood of the Vault, who were generally older than Hoagland and Appel's associates, the BUF sought to empower a less militant faction among the black community. Either way, as White would eventually concede, the fund-raising efforts amounted to little more than a "floral piece" in the guilt-ridden wake of the Kerner report and the murder of Martin Luther King.

If Mayor White was going to grant handouts, he also wanted to assure himself an image boost as a new kind of unity-fostering politician. On the twentieth of April, the mayor's office co-sponsored an all-day seminar on black employment with Roxbury church leaders. In a concluding address, White called for the facilitation of increased black entrepreneurship. That evening, he spoke at the eighty-first annual banquet of the *Harvard Law Review.* "Enrichment" programs, he said, while admirable, would have the adverse effect of keeping African-Americans relegated to the ghetto. The true solution, he said, was real integration. "The time has come for me after one hundred days in office, and for this nation after one hundred years, to put, as Lincoln did, the preservation of the Union above all else, the creation of a single society of white and black above all else."

James Brown was thinking of Lincoln, too. Dr. King, as the singer had noted in his televised address in Washington, was martyred just as Jesus Christ, President Lincoln, and President Kennedy had been before him. "This is a hard thing," Brown said in his extemporaneous remarks. "It's hard to digest. We all love Dr. Martin Luther King. I knew him personally, and he was a fine man. But he's a finer man now because he proved so many things."

Excerpts from Brown's speech were read into the Congressional Record twice that month, by New York senator Jacob Javits (with the performer repeatedly credited as "Jamie" Brown) on the day after King's funeral, and by Iowa congressman Fred Schwengel a few weeks later. "We wanted a hero, so we got one," Brown said. "We got something to live for. . . . We got a man of the world. We got a dream we want to fulfill. We can do more with that dream now than he ever did because we know what he left." For Brown, the primary concern was that the country's racial divide "don't cost no more lives."

"I'll be doing everything I can to make sure," he said, "and I—I might give my life."

In Memphis on the Monday after King's assassination, Coretta Scott King and her family led a silent march of nineteen thousand to honor her husband and reiterate support for the city's striking sanitation workers. King's body was brought to Georgia on a jet chartered by Robert Kennedy. At the church in Atlanta, Rev. Ralph Abernathy, King's right-hand man, called it "one of the darkest hours in the history of the black people of this nation . . . one of the darkest hours in the history of all mankind." Then he played a recording of King delivering his own eulogistic address at Ebenezer in February. In the speech, the minister acknowledged that one day he would be gone. In one of the most eloquent addresses of the master speaker's public life, he wished to be remembered, he said, as "a drum major for justice."

King spoke of the drum major's instinct to *be somebody*, and how all human beings crave praise and recognition. James Brown was a case study in this craving, a man who crafted his entire persona around the premise that he was surpassingly worthy of awe and admiration.

But as big as his ego was, he was unmistakably moved by the fact that his popularity afforded him the opportunity to try to do some good in the world. For Brown in 1968, it was showtime, and he knew it. Jesus, said King, was not opposed to the vanity of the drum-major instinct, as long as it was made useful. "He said in substance, 'Oh, I see, you want to be first. You want to be great. You want to be important. You want to be significant,' " the preacher pealed. " 'Well, you ought to be. If you're going to be my disciple, you must be.' But he reordered priorities. And he said, 'Yes, don't give up this instinct. It's a good instinct if you use it right. It's a good instinct if you don't distort it and pervert it. Don't give it up. Keep feeling the need for being important. Keep feeling the need for being first. But I want you to be first in love. I want you to be first in moral excellence. I want you to be first in generosity. That is what I want you to do.' "

Anticipating his own demise, King had asked that his eulogists ignore his accomplishments, his awards and degrees. "If you want to say that I was a drum major, say that I was a drum major for justice," he said. "Say that I was a drum major for peace. I was a drum major for righteousness. And all of the other shallow things will not matter."

★ ★ ★ 10 ★ ★ ★

IT'S A NEW DAY

Funerals were no place for James Brown. In life as in music, forward motion was, for him, the cardinal rule. He saw no point in looking back. "Every day is history to me," he once said. Brown's closest associates agree that he was superstitious about funerals. "In his mind," says one, "if he didn't see the casket lowered, the person wasn't gone."

It appears that James Brown told none of his closest companions about his plans to attend Dr. King's funeral in Atlanta on the ninth of April, 1968. His girlfriend, his bodyguard, and his personal assistant at the time all swear they have no recollection of him going.

Tens of thousands surrounded Ebenezer Baptist Church that day, listening over loudspeakers to the funeral service. The sheer-faced brick church at 407 Auburn Avenue, where King had served as co-pastor with his father, Martin Luther King, Sr., accommodated about eight hundred congregants. The guest list was formidable—the widows of Dr. King and President John F. Kennedy, Vice President Hubert Humphrey, presidential candidates including Richard Nixon and Robert F. Kennedy, and scores of congressmen, senators, mayors, governors, and civil rights leaders. They were joined by dozens of well-known entertainers and athletes, among them Harry Belafonte, Sammy Davis, Jr., Mahalia Jackson, Aretha Franklin, Diana Ross, Sidney Poitier, Paul Newman, Bill Russell, and Wilt Chamberlain.

In those years, wherever he went, James Brown drew a mob. The previous December, he had attended the service in Macon, Georgia, for his friend Otis Redding, after the singer's death in a plane crash. Brown's arrival had incited pandemonium. As fans surged forward, he had to dive for his car, and the driver could not follow the hearse until police forced back the onrushers. At King's funeral, James Brown—for once in his life—did not want to be noticed.

By 1968, Brown's voice was one of the most powerful in the country. "The hard, driving shouting of James Brown identifies a place and image in America," wrote the poet and cultural theorist Amiri Baraka, who was then LeRoi Jones, in 1966. "A people and an energy, harnessed and not harnessed by America. James Brown is straight out, open, and speaking from the most deeply religious people on this continent." To the poet, a jazz aficionado who was writing about the new relevance of soul music in the 1960s, Brown's scream, entrenched as it had become in the very center of mainstream culture, was still more radical than even the most revolutionary squawking of the free jazz experimentalists. "Certainly his sound is 'further out' than

Ornette's," Baraka argued. "And that sound has been a part of black music, even out in them backwoods churches since the year one."

But Brown, already more than a decade into his recording career, was just getting started. Nineteen sixty-eight would prove to be a mighty pivotal year for him—musically, personally, politically. Just as the King assassination would embody the terrible significance of the year, the course of Brown's own life would be drastically altered by the losses he would suffer, the scrutiny he would face, and the intense pressure he would put on himself in 1968.

Creatively, Brown was in the eye of a six-year storm. "Papa's Got a Brand New Bag," recorded and released in 1965, had been followed by more testaments to the band's collective dexterity such as "Cold Sweat," "Get It Together," and Brown's newest single, "I Got the Feelin'," another thriller marked by Bernard Odum's rutting bass playing, Clyde Stubblefield's fitful drumming, and the superheroic blams and ka-pows of Pee Wee Ellis's horn arrangement. But Brown's "new bag" also included a considerable share of hedge bets, including a cloying version of "The Christmas Song," a straightforward take on the old Leiber & Stoller rock 'n' roller "Kansas City," which maintained a prominent place on the nightly set list (in Boston, it followed "That's Life"), and "If I Ruled the World," which inaptly appeared in March as the B-side to the comparatively anarchic "I Got the Feelin'."

As adventurous as Brown's music was rapidly becoming, his sense of showmanship was still tethered to the Jazz Age razzle-dazzle of the Cotton Club, circa 1930. Midway through the Boston Garden show, in fact, Maceo Parker had mugged uncomfortably through the show's nightly comedy routine. By early 1968, the James Brown show was equal parts old-time vaudeville and stratospheric superfunk, a juxtaposition that only reinforced the notion that when the singer dropped into one of his seam-busting splits, he was straddling two worlds—the cultural conventions of Ed Sullivan and Dick Clark, and the futuristic blackness that would soon be adopted by electric-period Miles Davis and George Clinton's outlandish P-Funk bands.

As April descended, Brown was preparing his next two singles for release the following month. One, a two-part trance called "Licking Stick—Licking Stick," would be recorded in mid-April at King Studios. It would be the label's first release in stereo. The other was a holdover from a year-old session.

"America Is My Home" was unabashed jingoism, a veritable Uncle Sam recruiting poster and paternalistic rejoinder to the mounting complaints of the counterculture. "Name me any other country you can start out as a shoeshine boy and shake hands with the president," Brown dared, affixing as ever his own up-by-the-bootstraps mythos to the national promise of upward mobility.

"There's no country can beat us if we get the race problem fixed," the singer once said in the pages of *Billboard* magazine. "This is *home*. We can't leave. Never found another nation yet that could make hard ice cream or decent soul food." He was unapologetically patriotic, even in times when to be so was unstylish. As a child he deeply admired the moral showdowns of his beloved Hollywood Westerns, and he thought of himself as an American freedom fighter. "Unless you fight for your country you have nothing to fight for," he wrote on the inner gatefold of the album *Revolution of the Mind*, alongside a reproduced image of the Constitution.

In later years Brown made some effort to rescue "America Is My Home" from its critics by claiming, with its plainspoken rhymes and stream-of-consciousness thought process, that it was the first rap record—"I'm sorry for the man that don't love this land / Now black and white, they may fight, but if the enemy come, we'll get together and run 'em out of sight!" The tune, driven by the easy motor of Nolen's upstroke, was agreeable enough, but in the spring of 1968, the subject matter fell on deaf, if not openly hostile, ears. Anti-American sentiment was mushrooming, especially among a younger generation that would ensure the music industry a record-breaking billion-dollar gross for the calendar year. The official publication of the Kerner report had placed the blame for the social ills of the inner-city ghetto squarely at the feet of white America. Muhammad Ali was gaining support among the middle class as he approached his first full year of banishment from boxing, appealing his five-year prison sentence for draft evasion. And the Black Panthers had secured their place in the national debate on race relations, with Minister of Information Eldridge Cleaver set to embark on a presidential campaign under the banner of the Peace and Freedom Party. With an increasingly unpopular war escalating overseas and the country's domestic situation in crisis, few soul fans seemed interested in hearing James Brown declare "America Is My Home."

And yet the song—largely forgotten in the endless repackaging of Brown's vast catalog—did manage to climb to number thirteen on the R&B charts. Though it failed to crack the pop top forty, the surprising truth of its success among African-American audiences suggests two things: that black America was not as uniformly disinclined toward patriotism as historians have tended to assume, and that the song was hampered from greater success at least as much by its competition from the musically more dissident "Licking Stick" as it was by the disapproval of potential buyers. There's a third possible explanation, actually: By early 1968, James Brown was so popular with black Americans that he could have recorded "How Much Is That Doggie in the Window?" and sold records.

In any event, "Licking Stick" and "America Is My Home" were followed by perhaps the best-known phenomenon of Brown's fifty-year recording career. On the seventh of August, Brown and his band hastily reserved time for an evening session at Los Angeles's Vox Studios. The plan, typically, was to whip together a completed song from a snatch of rhythm, a horn riff from Pee Wee's seemingly bottomless supply, and a general lyrical topic around which Brown could brainstorm. The idea was to expand on a mantra Brown had instilled in the members of his entourage, reminding them that they should be proud of their heritage. It was a rhyming slogan that had been in casual use for some time in certain circles around the country, including the Bay Area's Afro-American Association (AAA): "Say It Loud—I'm Black and I'm Proud."

Brown wanted the song to be a joyful celebration of blackness, and he decided he wanted a chorus of children to deliver the refrain like a playground chant. As he would tell the story in later years, he sent Bobby Byrd out to a nearby Denny's restaurant to round up a group of adolescents who could respond to his call—"Say it loud!" (In other accounts, it was Charles Bobbit who rounded up the kids; the AAA's Donald Warden credits a third assistant, Brown's wardrobe mistress, Gertrude Saunders.) The children, Brown claimed, were not all black but a mix, including Asians and whites. The session was the first with Brown for new bassist "Sweet" Charles Sherrell. He says Brown was right: "It was just a bunch of kids. It wasn't like one origin, a bunch of black kids. That's the truth. I remember it because, by me being fresh in the band, only a couple of months, my eyes were wide open to everything."

The song was, and would remain, the most overt statement about the civil rights struggle Brown ever recorded. "We'd rather die on our feet than live on our knees," he famously brayed. Just months after King's murder, with revolution in the air both at home and abroad, "Say It Loud" was heard from most sides as a call to militancy. It was an immediate smash on soul stations, seizing the number-one spot on the R&B chart and retaining it for six weeks. In a season of blockbuster pop hits including "Hey Jude," "Love Child," and "Born to Be Wild," it reached the tenth spot on the pop chart as well.

King Records, sensing the song's urgency, rush-released it. Within three weeks of the recording session, audiences were already prepared to do their part in the most socially charged adaptation of traditional church call-and-response ever to hit the commercial marketplace. In Dallas, where the band recorded a live performance at the end of August (released years later as *Say It Live and Loud*), the ten-thousand-seat Memorial Auditorium began to rock as Brown introduced his new song. "If a man is not proud of who he is and where he come[s] from, he's not a man," he said. Then he kicked off the tune with a karate-chop cue.

"Unh!" he began, with Stubblefield crashing a cymbal in unison. "With your bad self!" Pee Wee Ellis's arrangement called for the horn players to throw an exploratory patter of notes, followed on the bridge by a decisive series of punches. It was the musical version of Ali, shuffling his feet as he met an opponent in the middle of the ring, feeling him out with jabs, and then whomping him with haymakers. If this was a celebration of blackness, its resolve was unmistakable.

The audience, as did audiences throughout the Southern swing that would take the band from Houston to Lafayette and Memphis in a matter of weeks that summer, shouted the refrain back at the band with an earth-shaking vigor. Having been on the bus for long stretches the past few weeks, the band was not fully aware of the wildfire success of the song. "To get that kind of reaction was mindblowing," says Ellis.

Black disc jockeys at the time were the popular voice of a people otherwise woefully underrepresented across the media landscape. Their enthusiasm for the song, as had been their support throughout Brown's career, was critical to its success. To his listeners, Brown's instantly classic opening gambit—"Unh! With your bad self"—was just as purposeful as the unambiguous instruction of the song's title. When the singer addressed his audience that way, said Jerry Bledsoe, otherwise known as Jerry B, one of the many well-known DJs on New York's WWRL-AM, one of the premier soul stations of the time, he was acknowledging his fellow man's struggle. "James Brown knows the problems we have," he said. "Mayor Lindsay is not saying 'with your bad self' to these people in Harlem."

In the late Rev. Jasper Williams's historical sermon "I'm Black and I'm Proud," recorded during a church service at Lane Avenue Baptist Church in Memphis not long after Brown's song was released, the preacher begins to draw his breath with an ominous, increasingly loud rattle in his throat as he works himself and his congregation into exultation. The sermon is an acknowledgment that James Brown's song "has captured the minds and attention particularly of our black children, and has given them something to cling to." In a litany of African-American heroes, including George Washington Carver (with his "brilliant mind"), Sister Rosa Parks, Jackie Robinson, and Joe Louis ("who could hit as hard as the clap of thunder"), Williams eventually settles on the biblical figure of Simon, the Cyrenian who helped Jesus bear the load of his cross. "It was a black man by the name of Simon that helped my Lord with his cross," Williams cries before inhaling another heaving lungful. "Remember now that the cross had the sins of the whole world in it." Thus the black man, says Williams, who ministered for years on WDIA, has suffered the sins of the modern world, sitting at the back of the bus, struggling for "first-class" jobs. "Don't be soft with it!" he roars, to shouts of encouragement. "Like the songwriter said, 'Say it loud.' "

The timing of the song was extraordinary. The civil rights movement was beginning to wane. Dr. King, of course, was gone, and no single leader was prepared to assume his galvanizing role. Black nationalist sentiment was on the rise, and, for many, the instinct toward separatism was understandable.[2] As Robert Kennedy had told a gasping crowd in Indianapolis upon delivering the news of King's murder, "For those of you who are black and are tempted to be filled with hatred and distrust at the injustice of such an act, against all white people, I can only say that I feel in my own heart the same kind of feeling."

[2] In his autobiography, Brown claimed that Otis Redding once approached him about forming a black entertainers' union. According to Brown, he told his friend, "I don't believe in separatism. I think that's going backwards, and I don't want to be part of that."

At the same time, the movement was faltering precisely because it had reached a previously unattainable plateau. The
Civil Rights Acts of 1957, 1964, and 1968 had secured unprecedented advances toward the end of Jim Crow discrimination
and the establishment of equal-opportunity employment. With
the passage of the Voting Rights Act of 1965, registration among
black Americans was at an all-time high, and African-American
politicians were beginning to fill some prestigious offices across
the nation. The identifying label black, once considered con-
descending, was poised to outdate the midcentury terms *Negro*
and *colored*, and "Say It Loud—I'm Black and I'm Proud" undoubtedly hastened the process. "I was the one who made the
dark-complexioned people popular," Brown would claim, with
characteristic self-assurance. After "Say It Loud" came out, "the
dark-skinned man had all of a sudden become cosmopolitan."

There were those, however, who felt the song was a face-saving
ploy for Brown, whose political involvement had attracted growing charges from black nationalists that he'd sold out. In later
years, Brown would claim that he received an ominous warning
in the form of a disabled grenade at the door of his hotel room
on the day of the recording; sidekick Hank Ballard sometimes
implied that the bandleader had been confronted by Black Panthers with machine guns at one show over his refusal to make
the lyrical content of his songs as revolutionary as the music.
"He got jacked up," as Marva Whitney claims.

There was, in fact, some history of black activists demanding
radicalism from black entertainers. "The Black Panthers hated
me because I supported Martin Luther King," Eartha Kitt once
said. "They threw stones at me when I appeared at the Apollo."
As Maulana Karenga (Ron Everett), the founder of the rival US

Organization, declared at the height of black nationalist sentiment, "All art must reflect the Black Revolution, and any art that does not discuss and contribute to the revolution is invalid." This idea could be traced all the way back to Du Bois, who once said, "I do not care a damn for any art that is not used for propaganda." (However, some of Brown's friends in the Afro-American Association have claimed that the real threats over "Say It Loud" actually came from the singer's manager, Ben Bart, who was reportedly vehemently opposed to the recording.)

In July, *Muhammad Speaks*, the weekly publication of Elijah Muhammad's Nation of Islam, had published a story bearing the headline, "Has James Brown Rejected His Black Supporters for White Recognition?" The article quoted at length from a letter written by a man named Frank Ochieng, identified as an African living in Cambridge, Massachusetts. His complaint involved the blunt patriotism of "America Is My Home." "There is no explanation as to why Brother Brown would record such propaganda," he wrote, "unless shaking hands with the president was his only ambition in life.

"Black youth have made him a hero," Ochieng wrote. "We realize that Brother Brown has contributed to 'the cause' in most cases generously. But what good is money without moral commitment?" Two months later Brown acknowledged the Nation of Islam's criticisms, placing a full-page advertisement in *Muhammad Speaks* for "Say It Loud." The ad featured the complete lyrics of the song and a simple message: "What many of us over the years have been ashamed to say is now being said with pride and dignity." The singer chose a smiling photo of himself alongside a sullen-looking David McCarthy, both in dark suits. McCarthy was identified as Brown's general manager.

Along with accountant Greg Moses, who was sometimes quoted in national publications about Brown's financial affairs, McCarthy was, in fact, a member of the Nation of Islam. Brown actually welcomed several members of the Nation into the fold over the years; Charles Bobbit, for instance, was known as Charles X when he joined the entourage. "He was our martial arts instructor," recalls photographer James Spencer, who answered to the name James Muhammad in the 1960s. Over the years Brown's band featured several practicing Muslims, including conga player Johnny Griggs and trumpeters Richard "Kush" Griffith, Darryl "Hasaan" Jamison, and Jerone "Jasaan" Sanford.

Brown respected the Nation's emphasis on self-discipline and was respectful of Elijah Muhammad, who, he understood, had a strong following among working-class African-Americans. (In fact, Brown's radio stations carried Muhammad's weekly address well into the 1970s.) "James Brown would always tell me that he respected Elijah Muhammad's self-help thing," says Al Sharpton, "but he didn't believe in the Muslim religion because he was a Christian."

Whatever the extent of his radical credentials, Brown's commitment to pacifying the riots ("Don't terrorize, organize," he'd become fond of reciting; "Don't burn, learn") made him a target of denunciation in some circles. In another gesture that stirred some controversy, the singer took his band to Vietnam in June to perform for the combat troops in and around Saigon. Only seven members of Brown's orchestra were allowed to make the trip with him. Marva Whitney, Brown's offstage companion (his first marriage, to Velma Warren in 1953, was effectively over by 1964), went, as did Stubblefield, Maceo Parker, Waymon Reed, St. Clair Pinckney, Jimmy Nolen, and newly hired bassist Tim

Drummond. (Bizarrely, in his slapdash 2005 memoir, *I Feel Good*, Brown claimed that all of the musicians he'd traveled with had passed away, including Drummond, certifiably alive at this writing, and "Clyde Shubble," also still alive.)

Ellis, the arranger, had been scheduled to go, but he was detained at the last minute after receiving a call from the FBI, who told him he couldn't go. The Bureau's decision stemmed from an eight-month incarceration he'd served in 1955. A white girl, a jazz groupie he'd been seeing in Rochester, turned out to be related to a local judge, who did not take kindly to this colored musician picking up with his niece. According to Ellis, this led to a bogus marijuana bust. Thirteen years later, the FBI cited the jail stint in order to prohibit him from traveling to Vietnam.

Brown had wanted to go to Vietnam for some time. Bob Hope, the perennial USO entertainer, was at the White House dinner Brown had attended in May; according to the singer, the comedian had agreed that Brown would have a receptive audience among the troops, a disproportionate number of whom were black. But Brown needed the intercession of John Johnson, the founder of *Jet* and *Ebony* magazines, to convince the government. In the end, the singer claimed to have paid his own way, and to have forgone $100,000 in canceled bookings in the process. "I knew that the black soldiers were complaining that the USO didn't send enough acts they could identify with," he would recall years later, "and I wanted to change that."

Joe Brown, James's father, had served in the Navy during World War II, stationed in Okinawa. That was where the Revue first landed, with Brown and his core group moving on to Saigon for a week of three-a-days. Designated as honorary lieutenant colonels, the entourage checked into the Continental Hotel, where the damage from January's Tet Offensive and the recent May Offensive was evident. Brown would recall the commotion from a mortar shell that killed seventeen near the hotel just a few hours before their arrival; during their stay the beds shook from overnight bombing raids by the Americans just outside the city. "In my room, the window was facing the President's palace," Drummond remembered. "It had a sign on it saying, 'Don't open the blinds with a light on behind you at night, [or] you will be shot as a sniper.' "

Drummond's stint with the group, which had begun just months before, was already nearing its conclusion. According to Charles Sherrell, Drummond came down with a case of hepatitis upon returning from Vietnam, and Sherrell, who had joined the Revue as an auxiliary drummer, was moved into the bassist's slot. But Drummond's brief presence was significant. Brown brought him in because he could perform—the bassist went on to a notable career as a session musician with Neil Young, Bob Dylan, and many others. But the hire was also intended as a symbolic gesture. When Drummond, the only white member of the group, ran into trouble at the Regal Theater in Chicago, where a staff member tried to tell him to leave the stage, Brown refused to comply, just as he had threatened to boycott segregated venues a few years before.

In the days of Black Nationalism, some interpreted the integration of Brown's band as another misstep for the singer, whose every move was now coming under scrutiny. Band members could see it on the faces of their black audiences: What was this white guy doing playing with James Brown?

Drummond, who by his own admission was "full of piss and vinegar" in those days, was determined to be a part of the group that went to Vietnam, to help make a statement about black and white relations. Given the volatile domestic situation in 1960s America, the troops in Vietnam faced a continuous undercurrent of racial tension among their own ranks. In Saigon—despite the nostalgic inference of Hollywood's Vietnam films, with their morale-boosting Motown soundtracks—popular music was often a matter of contention, with many white soldiers favoring country-and-western music and black soldiers preferring soul. "There were virtual riots over the music," historian Wallace Terry would report.

"The death of Martin Luther King created a lot of hostility," said Dave Gallaher, an infrared specialist with the Sixteenth TAC Recon Squadron, a white soldier who played guitar in an otherwise black group called the Rotations, covering R&B hits in the officers' clubs of Saigon. He caught Brown's show at one of two appearances in an air-conditioned theater at Tan Son Nhut Air Base. Drummond's presence, he felt, was exemplary: "I think James showing up with a white musician just put everyone on a little bit of notice about cooling out." In brutal heat that often exceeded 120 degrees, Brown and his players were required to wear fatigues en route to their appearances at the air bases at Tan Son Nhut and Phan Rang and the Bear Cat base of the Ninth Infantry, changing upon arrival into light, collarless indigenous shirts and, for Marva Whitney, a miniskirt. Soldiers with grenade launchers sat in the open doorway of their helicopter, searching for snipers. At Long Binh, performing for seven thousand troops in an overcrowded open-air amphitheater, Brown reacted to the sound of nearby artillery fire by breaking into a spontaneous rendition of "My Country 'Tis of Thee." At Bear Cat, the final performance of the week, tens of thousands of soldiers crowded around a hillside stage, many watching from the open hatches of their parked tanks, as if they were at a drive-in. "That was the best that band ever sounded," Drummond maintained, "stripped down like that."

Nearly two decades after the trip, Brown told the *Augusta Chronicle* that his USO tour was one of the most satisfying episodes of his life, regardless of the frightening proximity to live combat and the criticism the singer faced upon returning to America. "I was carrying the pride of America with me—the pride of humanity from free people throughout the world," he said. "I take pride in going anywhere to serve God and to try to soothe the savage beast in man."

Shortly after the fact, however, he was less interested in discussing the gesture than he was in protesting what he considered "fourth class" treatment by the military. The facilities were substandard; the allowance of only eight musicians was unforgivable. "What really hurt me was the fact we had two go-go dancers, which I'm sure the fellows wanted to see," he told a reporter from *Soul* magazine. "And they wouldn't let me carry a cameraman to take pictures and show what we were doing. I'm sure Bob Hope and John Wayne can do anything they want."

If Brown was speaking out more often, it was partly due to the fact that he was being invited to do so. In July, he appeared on the *Today* show, where he was interviewed at length about the state of black America. The following year he would make multiple appearances on the *Mike Douglas Show*, at one point engaging Alfred Hitchcock in a surreal discussion about the climactic scene in *Psycho* (which Brown mistakenly referred to as *Homicidal*). Did the director use a female stand-in for Anthony Perkins when he was dressed as his mother? Brown wanted to know. "I wouldn't dare tell you," Hitchcock teased. "That's worth money! Do you want to ruin me?" It was a reply that Brown, smiling broadly, could understand completely.

Brown reported the *Today* show appearance in his conversational new magazine column, "I'm Tellin' Ya!," in *Soul*, a Los Angeles-based weekly magazine covering the spectrum of black popular music. "It was a gas!" he wrote. He was beginning to feel like a "real expert" at navigating the formalities of talk-show television. "The only thing left for me to do now is a movie or a Broadway play," he wrote.

In September he used the column to clarify his role-model status. "I've been acting as a spokesman to my people," he wrote. "Keep in mind, I haven't been acting as a spokesman FOR my people—I'm not qualified to do that. I don't know who is." More often than not, the column was a hodgepodge of tour-diary entries, replies to readers' questions about his dance moves and his clothing style, gratuitous plugs for new recordings by Bobby Byrd, Marva Whitney, and other associates, and simplistic all-purpose advice ("I've found that if you just keep working and practicing and working some more, things are bound to get better"). Occasionally, however, he tackled weightier issues. In the column dated September ninth, he offered his perspective on black militancy: "There is no such thing as a militant. When a person is tired of being treated as a puppet, he is labeled a militant. Give him his rights and you will have no trouble with him." He also presented a list of "Black Commandments," a five-point program that began with the letters B, L, A, C, and K.

The final point read, "Knocking on the door has gotten boring and pathetic. We ARE coming in."

★ ★ ★ ❚❚ ★ ★ ★

IT'S TOO FUNKY IN HERE

For the King of Soul, the death of Dr. King inaugurated a long, trying season. The trip to Vietnam was arduous. "Say It Loud—I'm Black and I'm Proud," while a cultural triumph, coincidentally posed a commercial predicament for the singer. "A lot of people still didn't understand it," Brown would write. "They thought I was saying kill the honky."

Perhaps worst of all, some of his most devoted fans were threatening to abandon him over his political gestures and alliances. Though James Brown believed himself to be invulnerable, the criticism cut deeply. Those close to him knew that being called an Uncle Tom was an especially bitter pill for him to swallow.

At the end of May, Brown's idol, Little Willie John, died in Washington State Prison at Walla Walla of complications from pneumonia, a shell of a man at the stinging young age of thirty. Some months later Brown released his tribute album, *Thinking of Little Willie John . . . and a Few Nice Things.* But nice things were becoming harder for Brown to envision.

In Los Angeles in June, Brown sent newly hired advance man Bob Patton on an errand to the Ambassador Hotel to tell Robert Kennedy that the singer wanted to endorse his presidential candidacy. Kennedy told Patton, " 'Hey, that's great. He's a good man, a good American,' " says Patton. A few hours later, Kennedy lay mortally wounded in a kitchen passageway at the hotel.

Soon thereafter, Brown was waylaid by news of the death of Ben Bart, who collapsed of a heart attack while playing golf with his son. "Being from Georgia, Pop was the first white person we really felt comfortable with," Brown would write. "Usually, no matter what happens, I hold my grief in." But the death of his manager, coming just a few months after the passing of Mr. Nathan, made the battle-hardened entertainer break down and cry.

The loss of his manager coincided with the beginnings of financial-management issues that would hector the singer for the rest of his life. Brown was in fact estranged from Bart, who had essentially retired to a houseboat in Miami, at the time of the promoter's death. The two men were squabbling over their respective shares of the profits, with Bart eventually suing the singer.

Shortly after Bart's death, the IRS delivered its first of many letters to Brown, demanding the payment of nearly two million dollars in unpaid taxes. Running his operation on a cash-only basis, he would have a lifetime of problems with the federal government over his taxable earnings. In his autobiography, published in 1986, Brown would rather brazenly declare himself exempt from taxation. Without a proper education, he reasoned, "they have no legal boundaries over me. . . . You pay tax when you exercise all of your rights. I didn't exercise rights. I didn't have a chance to."

Oddly, too, in the year that he helped calm the riots in Boston and Washington, D.C., a disturbing number of Brown's concerts were still providing the setting for anarchy. Shows at Yankee Stadium and in Oakland were marred by violent outbreaks. (Before the Oakland show, Brown appeared on the San Francisco television program *Black Dignity*, hosted by Donald Warden and produced by Ed Howard.) At the Armory in Washington, D.C., an extended episode involving hundreds of ticketholders culminated with a fast-spreading rumor that Brown had been killed by a white gunman. WOL was obliged to track down the singer in California the next day so he could assure fans he was still alive. Rumors such as this were becoming routine.

After the assassination of Robert Kennedy, Brown came out in support of Hubert Humphrey. At an early summer rally in a Los Angeles parking lot where a grocery store had burned during the Watts riots, Brown addressed an audience of several hundred young people representing the Watts Labor Community Action Committee's summer program. He spoke like a man seeking a nomination of his own. Voicing his concerns for the problems facing black neighborhoods, he explained that he endorsed "all black candidates so that we can have a representative voice in our government on all levels—local, state, and federal." Then he announced his intention to make "overtures to the gentleman on my right, to see how he responds." Humphrey, who had endured a hostile reception from a local crowd two days earlier, was apprehensive as Brown began calling for more black ownership and more low-income housing, "so we don't have to stay in the dumps like I stayed in as a kid." Next, the singer asked for a pledge to build more hospitals, "so we don't have to stand around and bleed to death." And he pressed for more black-oriented institutions, such as banks and hotels.

"The candidate that gives me those things, that's the man I endorse," he said. "I don't endorse the party—I endorse the man." A visibly relieved Humphrey—these were, after all, common-sense proposals for the betterment of black America—agreed, and the two unlikely allies clasped hands and broke into a spontaneous celebration dance. When Humphrey fumbled the words to "I Got You (I Feel Good)," Brown goaded him: "You got to have soul!" he hollered. To Robert Farris Thompson, this was a defining moment in Humphrey's ill-destined campaign. Humphrey, he told Brown biographer Cynthia Rose, lacked any "sense of resynchronizing his body language to this . . . *volcano* next to him. If ever there was a moment to tell you Humphrey was a loser, that was it." It was, in Thompson's words, "the style of James Brown in all-out confrontation with the straightest of white America."

In Boston, Kevin White was enduring problems of his own. Inspired in part by the success of the Boston Garden show, the mayor's administration was about to unveil a cultural outreach program called Summerthing. Looking to expand Boston's existing summertime arts festival, a highbrow affair located exclusively downtown, Summerthing director Katherine Kane and her colleagues consulted with officials from Carl Stokes's administration in Cleveland, which had established its own model arts festival.

Summerthing, however, was destined for a rough beginning. An opening-night appearance early in the summer of 1968 by

Smokey Robinson and the Miracles at the South End's Carter Playground, near Northeastern University, drew thousands more than anticipated. According to David Atwood, who was there supervising a remote feed for WGBH, the rented public address system never arrived, and the group was forced to perform without adequate amplification. The crowd was hostile, at one point turning over a parked car and setting it on fire. Atwood himself was menaced by a knife-wielding youth.

Still, Summerthing, with its live music events, its theater and ballet workshops, its Jazzmobile, and other programs, would become a symbolic cornerstone of White's early administration. Like James Brown, Kevin White had a pronounced flair for showmanship. Opposing the corrosive Louise Day Hicks, who would achieve national infamy during Boston's grinding busing crisis of the mid-1970s, White had been elected as the candidate most likely to keep the peace in a major American city at a time of racial strife. After initially supporting the decision to cancel Brown's Boston Garden concert, the mayor had managed to present himself as an ally of the most popular black entertainer of the day. Summerthing was a prime example of White's instinctive belief that it was the circuses, as much as the bread, that would carry the city out of despair. "He had invented celebrations as Fiedler invented the Pops, at least as far as staid and stodgy, dour old Boston was concerned," George Higgins would write in *Style Versus Substance: Boston, Kevin White, and the Politics of Illusion.* When the Rolling Stones were detained from a 1972 Boston Garden appearance by an arrest after an altercation in Rhode Island, White charged to the rescue, securing the band's release and arranging a high-speed state police escort. Long after Stevie Wonder had finished his opening set, the mayor triumphantly introduced the Stones at 12:45 in the morning.

The mayor's intuition for the stage would briefly propel him into the 1972 presidential campaign, when George McGovern considered choosing White as his running mate. But White's local support had been eroding since 1970, when his gubernatorial run had taken many backers by surprise. Some of his detractors felt he was too dependent on glamorous diversions, at the expense of real solutions to real problems. The mayor's national ambitions were laid to rest by the objections of key policymakers from his own home state, rumored among them Senator Ted Kennedy, economist John Kenneth Galbraith, and Congressman Robert Drinan. The last, a Jesuit priest, reportedly ridiculed White's proposed inclusion on the ticket by joking, "Whoever it was appeared to have the same name as the mayor of Boston." (White's removal from consideration, as Hunter S. Thompson maintained, had the unfortunate effect of instigating the "desperate grab-bag trip that eventually coughed up [Thomas] Eagleton," the Missouri senator whose history of receiving electric shock therapy would put a fatal nail in McGovern's own political coffin.)

Boston's ugly school-desegregation busing incidents of the 1970s would make an unfortunate mockery of White's aspirations. By mid-decade, with the city preparing to take center stage in the national bicentennial celebration, the mayor was badly in need of a hit. The shocking antagonisms of the busing crisis had exposed the old city, as Bill Russell once put it, as a "flea market of racism," dominated by a patronizing upper crust and an Irish-Catholic working class "ready to pick your fillings if you weren't the right religion or from the right clique—much less from the right race." By his last two terms, following the elections of 1975 and 1979, White was embattled and embittered by the city's factional infighting. No longer was he recognized as an innovative neighborhood coordinator. The "Little City Halls" were closed. Some of the same critics who had once accused him of excessive capitulation to the Roxbury activists, calling him Mayor Black, were now condemning his clampdown. He had, he said, an obligation to "orchestrate the city" during its time of crisis. That drive provided him with a new nickname—"King Kevin." By the dawn of the 1980s, the *Globe* was actively calling for him not to run again. "White has survived less because of political and more because of theatrical skills," the paper editorialized. "He has become the Marlon Brando of politics. His brush with Potomac fever a decade ago was his *On the Waterfront.*"

For a brief moment, though, in one of the most unlikely pairings to come out of the civil rights era, Kevin White and James Brown had been united onstage. "I never met anything like James Brown," the mayor would recall. "Man, he was a piece of work." For one extraordinary night, these two very different men were a couple of swingin' cats, coolly asking for cool heads to prevail in the almost unbearable aftermath of the murder that effectively ended the movement.

★ ★ ★ 12 ★ ★ ★

REALITY

Legend has it that the Last Poets formed in New York on Malcolm X's birthday, May 19, 1968. Two years later, the original trio released an album of stark, defiant performance poetry as the soundtrack to a film called *Right On!* A highlight of the album was the track "James Brown," on which the forceful frontman Gylan Kain implores the singer to cry, scream, sweat for his fellow man. "Cry, Jimmy, cry," Kain roars, spittle spraying. "Cry the pain of broken men that stumble past empty dreams." Brown, the poet attests to the accompaniment of measured hand claps and hypnotic conga drumming, is a "witch doctor," a "healer." To a group formed in Harlem's Marcus Garvey Park, Brown was an indispensible, superhuman figure. They needed him to leap tall buildings, to keep up his invincible act on their behalf: "Jimmy, don't fall!" Kain cries. "Please don't fall." His colleagues join the appeal: "Please . . .

please . . . please . . . please . . . *please please please please please please please please!"*

By 1970, they knew it was coming. Like just about every other politically charged figure of the 1960s, James Brown was, in fact, headed for a fall. Like any other power-hungry autocrat, he was destined to watch his empire erode. And like any other creative mastermind, his burning desire to show something new to the world would inevitably be supplanted by an increasingly desperate urge simply not to lose what he had gained.

The fall, however, would happen in slow motion, and for some time it appeared that he was still soaring. Nineteen sixty-nine, in fact, would begin with an anointment of sorts: Was James Brown "the most important black man in America?" In an age "when millions of hyper-aware young men and women wonder whether it is still possible to be both black and American," Thomas Barry wrote in *Look* magazine, Brown's constituency "dwarfs Stokely Carmichael's and the late Dr. Martin Luther King's." In the article, a Georgia policeman praised the singer's authority—"One gesture from him is worth one hundred cops"—and an Ohio disc jockey attested, "To me, personally, he represents what Malcolm X represented—he makes a black person feel like a man."[3]

"All I want for everybody is peace and understanding," Brown

[3] Such persuasion apparently led to extensive FBI surveillance of the singer. While published reports of James Brown's existing FBI file have featured records pertaining to his 1988 arrest, an exhaustive series of appeals under the Freedom of Information Act conducted during the writing of this book ultimately yielded a confirmation by the FBI that the bureau's Atlanta, Birmingham, and Baltimore field offices may have conducted much earlier surveillance on the singer, and that file records on Brown were destroyed according to maintenance schedules in June 1989, and July 2001.

sang that year, stretching out the word pee-ee-eace like a death rattle, on one distressed message song, "I'm Not Demanding."

His heightened profile converted naturally into cultural capital. "Give It Up or Turnit a Loose," "I Don't Want Nobody to Give Me Nothing (Open Up the Door I'll Get It Myself)," and "Mother Popcorn" were all R&B smashes (two of them number ones) that also made the pop top twenty. Before playing Madison Square Garden, the singer placed big ads in New York newspapers touting his brand of black power—"the kind that is achieved not through the muzzle of a rifle but through education and economic leverage." After supporting Humphrey during the 1968 campaign, Brown opened the new year by playing one of Richard Nixon's inaugural balls, sharing a bill with Duke Ellington, Lionel Hampton, and the classical pianist Andre Watts. Though the singer later claimed he performed "Say It Loud—I'm Black and I'm Proud" for the Washington swells, band members maintain he stuck to less inflammatory material such as "If I Ruled the World" and "It's a Man's Man's Man's World."

Also in January, Brown released the first of two novelty records using a rudimentary form of sampling known as the "break-in," with a narrative spliced together from snatches of his own hit songs. The second of these singles, released in early 1970, was called "Soul President." Throughout his life Brown was fixated on the iconography of the American presidency, which, as every schoolboy knows, is the highest peak of upward mobility. One of Brown's most cherished possessions was the place card that Lyndon Johnson left for the entertainer at a White House dinner honoring the prime minister of Thailand in 1968, shortly after the King assassination. "Thanks much for what you are doing for your country—LBJ," the president had written.

"Brown used to show everyone all his commendations," says Jack Bart. "He'd say, 'This is a letter from Gerald Ford to me. Jack, do you have anything like that?' "

Though Nixon was vilified by much of black America for his divisive, politically expedient "Southern strategy" and his sustenance of the unpopular war in Vietnam, Brown endorsed him in 1972, prompting more protests that Soul Brother Number One had become a "Sold Brother." But Nixon had earned the support of other leading cultural figures, such as James Meredith, Jackie Robinson, and football star Jim Brown, with his economic initiatives. Campaigning before his first election to the White House in 1968, the son of a "nickel and dime" grocer had proposed a program called "Bridges to Human Dignity," which would offer not dependence but "a piece of the action" for the working class. During his tenure as president Nixon expanded affirmative action, proposed a guaranteed income, and established the Office of Minority Business Enterprise, acting on his campaign promise to increase "black ownership . . . black pride, black jobs, black opportunity, and yes, black power in the best, the [most] constructive sense of that often misapplied term." Though Brown's support of Nixon perplexed some of his closest friends, he refused to regret it.

Brown's "sepia Sinatra" foray into the Great American Songbook was in full swing in 1969, with the release of *Gettin' Down to It*, an acoustic jazz outing backed by Cincinnati's Dee Felice Trio which featured "That's Life" and "Strangers in the Night." At the end of the year he would record a big-band record, *Soul on Top*, in Hollywood with drummer Louis Bellson and arranger Oliver Nelson. Amid covers of Hank Williams's "Your

Cheatin' Heart" and another Leslie Bricusse number associated with Sammy Davis, Jr., "What Kind of Fool Am I?," as well as reinventions of "Man's World" and "Brand New Bag," the highlight was probably Brown's take on Bellson's own "I Need Your Key (to Turn Me On)." In an inspired spoken segment over the bridge, the singer extemporizes on *ki*, the Eastern power of positive thinking and mind-body synchronization. "Ki is the inner strength," Brown sermonizes with a "ha!," clearly enjoying himself. It "unlocks everything, and when it does—look out!"

But if he was still feeling it on the inside, outside forces were undoubtedly taking their toll. Among other things, the year brought a paternity suit, the departures of Pee Wee Ellis and Ms. Whitney (who would sing, at Brown's request, at his funeral), and racist opposition to Brown's purchase of a home in an upscale section of Augusta, where the singer would eventually move with his soon-to-be second wife, Deedee. In Los Angeles for a show at the Forum, Brown was invited to the office of Mayor Sam Yorty for a ceremony in which he was to receive a proclamation. But "Ramblin' Sam," as the mayor was known, was suddenly unavailable, so the task of greeting the singer fell to Deputy Mayor Joe Quinn. When he, too, failed to show, Brown felt compelled to complain in the press. "I believe in the dignity of man," he said. "I'm a busy man. I was here at the appointed time."

In May 1970, Brown's adopted hometown had a riot of its own, as a protest over the beating death of a jailed sixteen-year-old grew violent in Augusta. Georgia Governor Lester Maddox sent in the National Guard, and then he contacted the inner-city ambassador: He called James Brown. The singer flew back after an appearance in Michigan and went to his old house, which he'd given to his father. Meeting with the sheriff, he made plans to tour the burning neighborhood but declined to do it in a police cruiser. "That'll just make people madder," he said.

Over the course of several days, in the streets and over the airwaves from his own radio station, WRDW, and a competitor, WBBQ, the singer implored his fellow Augustans to stop the destruction. Relying on R&B stations to reach black communities in times of crisis was a time-tested practice; in Atlanta, Dr. King himself had a direct pipeline, with his SCLC office sharing a building with WERD, one floor below the studio. The black radio pioneer "Jockey" Jack Gibson recalled lowering his microphone out the window for the reverend whenever he needed to address the neighborhood.

"I tried to make the same point I made in Boston and Washington," Brown would remember, "that it didn't make sense to burn up your own neighborhood. 'This is your city, too,' I said. 'This country is as much yours as it is the white man's. Don't let anybody tell you it's not.' "

When Maddox, who came to office in 1967 a noted segregationist, suggested to Brown, "I don't know of anyone who is forcing unequal rights on your people," Brown was quick to disagree. "I'm from Augusta," he retorted. "People here don't have equality." Yet despite their differences, in time the two men would come to a mutual understanding, even an unlikely friendship. "I'd like to think that our getting to know each other," Brown would recall, "was as much a revelation for him as it was for me." Nixon, Ford, Reagan, George Wallace: Brown got a peculiar charge out of fraternizing with powerful men with whom he seemed to have little in common. When *Rolling Stone* asked the singer to name a great twentieth-century hero, he chose Strom

Thurmond, the South Carolina senator whose record-breaking filibuster nearly derailed the Civil Rights Act of 1957. (Weirdly, after Brown's death the late Thurmond's ancestors were found to have been the slaveowners of some of Al Sharpton's ancestors.)

"Presidents, secretaries of state, governors, mayors—I can honestly say I have never seen anybody dominate a meeting with James Brown," says Sharpton. "He talked to them like he'd talk to the average person on the street."

He had a harder time communicating democratically with the long-suffering musicians in his band. "He would chastise and counsel his employees in front of certain disc jockeys, reporters, and local politicians to make himself look benevolent and merciful, so many people actually thought him to be a leader and father figure," Fred Wesley recalled. "He was a master of manipulation." When the majority of Brown's definitive late-1960s band departed en masse in early 1970 in a dispute over salary cuts, Wesley, one of the few holdovers, stepped in as bandleader for an untested Cincinnati band called the Pacesetters, featuring future funk star William "Bootsy" Collins on bass and his brother, "Catfish," on guitar. Two holdovers—Bobby Byrd, playing organ, and Jabo (John Starks), Stubblefield's tag-team partner, on the drums—helped ease the transition for the Collins brothers, a new set of horn players, and conga player Johnny Griggs. In a single frenetic year at the beginning of the new decade, the reconstituted band, now called the J.B.s, propelled Brown through the most intense creative period of his career, recording such improvisational jams as "Get Up (I Feel Like Being a) Sex Machine," "Get Up, Get Into It, and Get Involved," and an effervescent invitation to mind your own business, "Talkin' Loud & Sayin' Nothing."

The big lineup had always been in flux, but in the new decade it was a veritable midway of comings and goings. Bootsy opened what would become a direct pipeline to George Clinton's carnivalesque Parliament-Funkadelic universe, where Wesley, Maceo, and trumpeter Richard "Kush" Griffith would all soon migrate. Meanwhile, Stubblefield and Nolen would wander back in, and St. Clair Pinckney, one of Brown's oldest running partners, came back to stay. Even Ellis, who had been one of the few to truly stand up to the boss, would drop in for a few sessions in 1973 and '74. There had been multiple layers of control issues underlying Pee Wee's departure as bandleader in 1969. From gig to gig, Ellis would "fly, or rent a car—not go on the bus. For some reason, that ticked [Brown] off." When Brown told him to stop traveling on his own or he'd be fired, Ellis took the bait. "I called my travel agent and said, 'Book a flight.' "

After nearly four years of pushing the band to the outer edges of soul without receiving what he felt was sufficient recognition, the easygoing Ellis was ready to step out from under the Cuban heel of the Godfather. He assembled a short-lived, racially mixed funk-rock group called Gotham, which signed to Motown's Natural Resources imprint. But the group, despite modeling itself after the commercially oriented Blood, Sweat & Tears, proved too artistically stubborn for its producers, and its run was brief. Relocated to the San Francisco Bay Area, Ellis developed a relationship with Van Morrison, for whom he served as arranger from 1979 to '85. Around the conclusion of his work with Morrison, the saxophonist crossed paths again with Brown. Brown, he says, gave him a backhanded compliment when he announced to the people in his dressing room, "See, Pee Wee is the only one who never came back."

As Brown's drawing power and his record sales began to dip, he clung ever more fiercely to his mountaintop. Although he reportedly remained the highest-paid black entertainer for the year 1971, his move to Polydor, after an exhausting fifteen-year climb to pop supremacy with King Records, would in retrospect mark the beginning of his descent. Brown's label switch coincided with soul music's blaxploitation infatuation—the wah-wah music that accompanied Hollywood's brief vogue with the African-American anti-hero. Brown, accustomed to being the trailblazer, suddenly found himself trailing Isaac Hayes, Curtis Mayfield, Marvin Gaye, and other, smoother soul brothers into the soundtrack business.

The film that signalled his introduction to the field, *Black Caesar*, starring former pro football star Fred Williamson, was envisioned as an African-American version of *The Godfather*. (Williamson's character, a onetime shoeshine boy who rose to become the "Godfather of Harlem," was the inspiration for what would become one of Brown's most indelible nicknames, "The Godfather of Soul.") The singer's next venture into the movies, for which he relied heavily on the arranging talents of Fred Wesley, was *Slaughter's Big Rip-Off*. It featured Jim Brown (who would soon become, like Williamson, a *Playgirl* pinup) in another mediocre crime-does-pay screenplay summarized by a comically melodramatic tagline: "The Mob put the finger on Slaughter, so he gave them the finger right back—curled tight around a trigger!"

As the undeniable glamour of the Black Power movement found a commercial outlet in the black action films of the early 1970s, its criminal element seemingly ran counter to Brown's own law-and-order bearing. But Hollywood had always been in the business of parsing moral ambiguities. Lover of Westerns that the singer was, he understood completely the emotions behind "an eye for an eye." Brown saw no conflict in being both a role model and a motherfucker. He was "Super Bad," and he felt nice, "like sugar and spice." With his whole identity wrapped up in his success in the marketplace, he wanted it—he demanded the right to have it—both ways.

After almost two decades of delivering hits the way Detroit delivered cars, Brown's three number ones on the R&B charts in 1974 would prove to be a last flurry of real relevance. One of them was called "The Payback," an uncharacteristically bitter (if widely influential—the rappers Ice-T and Ice Cube have both called it the prototypical gangsta rap) song that called for revenge. "I'm mad!" Brown barked. The *Payback* album, released in early 1974, hot on the heels of *Black Caesar* and *Slaughter*, had been commissioned as the soundtrack to *Hell Up in Harlem*, director Larry Cohen's sequel to *Caesar*. "Can you make it mellow, Fred?" Brown sings near the end of the surprisingly languid, essentially directionless "Doing the Best I Can." That song may have helped persuade Cohen that this new music was "not James Brown enough." The director rejected the sessions, turning instead to Edwin Starr, the second-tier Motown singer whose anti-Vietnam anthem "War" had been a huge number-one hit in 1970.

The slashing menace of "The Payback" can certainly be heard as Brown's vengeance for being turned down. More likely, however, it was about his anger over his mounting financial troubles. By this time the IRS was leaning on him for more than $4 million in unpaid taxes. "Save our money, like the Mob," he taunted on another 1974 single, "Funky President." Like a Mafia capo who arranges financial support for the extended families of his neighborhood, Brown still considered the example of his earning power to be his great contribution to black America.

Nineteen seventy-three was another difficult year for the entertainer. His support of Richard Nixon drew sustained outrage from some fans. At the Apollo, he faced signs reading JAMES BROWN, NIXON'S CLOWN. *Variety*, covering an earlier incident in Baltimore during the presidential campaign, reported that the concert was picketed and that Brown attracted only a fraction of the Civic Center's thirteen thousand capacity. It was, the magazine suggested, "a lesson to those performers who feel it necessary to declare themselv[e]s politically."

"You always risk losing money when you speak out," reflected Jim Brown, who, like his namesake, supported Nixon. "You had a choice of opening your mouth and maintaining your dignity or closing your mouth and keeping your money."

In May, following a weeklong run at the Apollo, Brown checked himself into a hospital in Jamaica, Queens, suffering from exhaustion. A month later his first son, Teddy Brown, was dead, killed in a car crash in upstate New York.

"Time Is Running Out Fast," as the title of one instrumental track from *The Payback* fretted. The song itself seemed self-refuting, loping along for a seemingly endless thirteen minutes. But the tolls—of impending middle age in a young man's business, of repeated infidelities, of financial promiscuity, of simply sticking his neck out—were finally dragging down a remarkable career. The late-1974 singles "My Thang" and "Papa Don't Take No Mess, Part 1" would prove to be the singer's final two top-forty entries (not counting the 1986 comeback anomaly

"Living in America"). Both songs appeared on the aptly titled *Hell* album.

Brown did manage to hang around the R&B charts on behalf of Polydor until the end of the decade, claiming a piece of the era's lighted dancefloors with songs such as "Hustle!!! (Dead On It)," "Get Up Offa That Thing," and "It's Too Funky in Here." By the time of his cameo appearance as the Rev. Cleophus James in *The Blues Brothers* (1980), however, he was, to the *Saturday Night Live* audience that worshipped the antics of young comedians Dan Aykroyd and John Belushi, that soul-crushing ignominy— an oldies act.

★ ★ ★ 13 ★ ★ ★

UNITY, PT. 1

"**P**eople wear leaders out," as Rev. Samuel Kyles once said of his deceased colleague, Martin Luther King, Jr. "If you do fifteen years, you're doing good."

In 1981, James Brown was celebrating his twenty-fifth year in popular music. It had been fifteen years since he'd launched his education crusade and appeared in Mississippi on behalf of James Meredith. In that time he had taken the concerns of the everyday Americans who made up his fan base—"My music tells what the man on the street feels," he once said—directly to the White House, the Queen of England, and the Pope. "A hundred years from now," one Black Arts writer once predicted, "if people want to find out what black people were in this country they will be listening to James Brown's records rather than reading Ralph Ellison."

In San Francisco in 1998, the singer stood outside a former

vaudeville theater, signing autographs. "Music is the soul of the people," he said. "That's why I'm the Godfather of Soul. I wouldn't want to be anything else—wouldn't want to be a king, or an emperor. I just want to be with the people."

He was the Muhammad Ali of music. "I had to prove you could be a new kind of black man," Ali explained. "I had to show the world." Over the years Ali and Brown had become mutual admirers, often engaging in good-natured competition to see who could draw the most attention on the city streets where their paths crossed. In 1974 Brown had been the marquee attraction at the "Rumble in the Jungle," promoter Don King's gala staging of the historic Ali–George Foreman title fight in Kinshasa, Zaire. Despite the delirium Brown caused with his performance at the so-called "African Woodstock"—which also featured the Spinners, B.B. King, and Bill Withers—that preceded the fight, the singer insisted on leaving the country before the contest began. He had engagements to honor, more money to make. His instinct had been validated when Zairean dictator Mobutu Sese Seko detained the other Americans after Ali's victory, in a dispute over the $10 million he had guaranteed the fighters.

By the summer of 1981, Ali was himself in decline, having lost to the new heavyweight champion, Larry Holmes, his former sparring partner, the previous year. He was already showing signs of the onset of Parkinson's disease as he prepared for his final professional bout, a loss to Trevor Berbick in December in the Bahamas. If Ali and Brown were reluctantly relinquishing their crowns, they remained iconic figures with enormous appeal. At the beginning of the summer they were invited to appear together on Tom Snyder's late-night talk show. The host wanted to talk about the looming possibility of another "long, hot summer" of race- and class-based tension. Snyder's staff, however, had evidently neglected to inform these two proud men of the night's subject, and they appeared caught off-guard. Though Studio 54 was then closed, Brown was dressed for it, wearing a straw cowboy hat pulled low over his brow; his otherwise bare torso was draped in a denim vest. To his right sat Ali, in a suit and tie; to his left sat a youthful Al Sharpton, also wearing a suit. When the host asked whether the situation at the onset of the economically precarious summer of 1981 might not be considered "hopeless," Brown just shook his head.

"It's never hopeless," he retorted. "No such thing as hopeless."

For Brown, however, it came perilously close. The last two decades or so of his life can be reduced to a disappointing series of snapshots, or rather, mug shots. Behind closed doors, this man of immaculate presentation and militant self-respect had been stowing some serious personal problems. "Mr. Brown thought he could influence people to be better," says Curtis Gibson, who became Brown's personal tailor in 1973. "But ninety percent of the time, when he was talking to the folks, he was talking to himself, too. And he couldn't do it."

With his third wife, Adrienne Rodriguez, the singer drew unwanted attention in several widely publicized episodes of domestic violence. "Adrienne used to wear her dark sunglasses quite often," says Jack Bart, Brown's booking agent until 2001. And close associates say the frontman famous for fining his musicians for drinking or smoking dope on the job had developed a secret dependency on the powerful psychoactive drug known as PCP. At a concert in Bern, Switzerland, the singer narrowly escaped arrest when Bart, alerted to the presence of a police patrol with a drug-sniffing dog, dumped a bottle of Brown's liquid PCP down the toilet in his dressing room. Bart says he was afraid to turn on the radio in the morning, fearing another arrest report. "The guy was constantly in trouble," he says.

The intense pressure Brown put on himself to build an empire and preach from its pulpit eventually—inevitably—became too great a burden. "It can be pretty scary up where I am," as he once told Doon Arbus, daughter of the photographer Diane, in a rare moment of candor. "I've got a lot of problems. I'm real confused, you know. But I gotta keep it all to myself. All inside me. 'Cause there ain't no one I can really talk to."

Like his private life, Brown's public presence was growing increasingly bizarre. When his ten-year Polydor contract lapsed in 1981, the singer made a partially successful effort to stay current with the Scotti Brothers, a pair of entrepreneurs from Newark who had broken into the music business with the teen idol Leif Garrett. Ben Scotti was a former NFL player whose claim to fame was a 1963 locker-room brawl with a Philadelphia Eagles teammate on the weekend following the assassination of President Kennedy. Ben Scotti and his brother, onetime actor Tony Scotti, went on to help launch the career of the song parodist "Weird Al" Yankovic and produce the television series *Baywatch*, among other ventures.

With the Scottis, Brown parlayed a kitschy appearance in *Rocky IV*, presiding over the spectacle of Apollo Creed's star-spangled entrance into the boxing ring, into a surprise top-ten showing for the comeback song "Living in America," written by a hired team that included the pop star Dan Hartman. For the creator of soul pride, it was an empty victory.

"How Do You Stop," he asked on one of his last songs to earn airplay. In 1988, Brown finally succeeded in upending his career when he was arrested in an exceptionally strange incident in which, reportedly under the influence of PCP, he threatened participants in an insurance-licensing seminar who were using a meeting room at his Top Notch office complex in Augusta. When police arrived, he led them on a wild highway chase, speeding around a roadblock before officers shot out the tires of his red and white Ford pickup truck. Convicted of carrying an unlicensed firearm and assaulting a police officer, among other offenses, the self-professed "model man" served twenty-six months of two concurrent six-year sentences in South Carolina prisons.

Rigid moralists, as Brown undeniably was during his years of peak production, are notorious backsliders. The indiscretions of lawmakers and clergymen—these discoveries never cease to confound the public, even as they continue to suggest an age-old pattern of human behavior. Brown, of course—the Soul President, the Minister of the New New Super Heavy Funk—identified closely with politicians and preachers alike. The same qualities that made him perfectly suited to cut through the despair following the murder of Dr. King—the sense that he was exemplary and invulnerable—were the qualities that would bring him down.

After serving his prison term, Brown's efforts at social engagement were often openly ridiculed. In May 2001, the mayor of Cincinnati made a desperate call to Brown. Following the shooting death of an unarmed nineteen-year-old black man by police, the most recent of several such incidents in the city, the home of King Records broke out in rioting. Cincinnati's annual Memorial Day weekend festival was in danger of becoming a public relations nightmare; black acts including the Isley Brothers backed out of scheduled appearances. In a move later characterized by Charles Bobbit as "a repeat of 1968—Boston, Massachusetts," Brown agreed to come. But boycott organizers were dismayed: The city, said Rev. Damon Lynch III, believed that "if we can just . . . get the Negro dancin', he'll forget about his anger, he'll forget about his pain." When Brown attempted to perform his new song, an anti-violence diatribe called "Killing Is Out, School Is In," he was hounded off the stage by protesters. "Bring Elvis back—they both dead now," hollered an old man.

If he heard it, Brown refused to acknowledge it. A few weeks later, he was at the White House, presenting President Bush with a T-shirt bearing the name of his new song.

Rare is the pop entertainer who can carry an audience over multiple decades. Rarer still is the pop star who can sustain any kind of long-term social relevance. With his unapologetic blackness, his radical musicality, and his vision of a global audience, James Brown was uniquely primed for the spotlight in the aftermath of the death of Martin Luther King. Years after the moment in which all the considerable powers of James Brown—musical, cultural, mythological—were aligned, the singer still believed himself to be a man with a message.

In January 1981, Brown was asked to perform at Ronald Reagan's inauguration; he declined. At his office complex, according to Al Sharpton, Brown had instructed the reverend to call the White House and ask how much he'd be paid. When the scheduler explained that it should be considered an honor to be asked to perform, Sharpton's mentor grabbed the phone and said, "Sir, this is James Brown. Ain't no honor for no black man to work for no money."

Shortly thereafter, in the same Augusta office, Sharpton and Brown sat discussing Stevie Wonder's tribute to Dr. King, "Happy Birthday," and the singer's plans to rally with Jesse Jackson for the establishment of a federal holiday for the slain civil rights leader. Despite a petition signed by six million supporters of the bill that would make the King holiday a federal law, the new president opposed it. Brown decided to make his own appeal. "I don't need to march," he told Sharpton. "I can call him. Get him on the phone."

"I said, yeah, right," recalls Sharpton, still laughing at the memory. He called; to Sharpton's amazement, the White House called back and asked James Brown to come see the president and Vice President George Bush on the fifteenth of January, King's birthday. Photos from the meeting feature Brown with Bush, but he also met with Reagan. Brown, Sharpton says, took the opportunity to engage the president in a one-sided debate. "He sat there and told Reagan, 'You're blowing the whole country.' Just like that!" The reverend, who had balked at speaking with Reagan, was dumbstruck: "I'm sitting there, I'm the ultimate activist—in those days, revolutionary—and I'm like, 'I don't believe he's telling the president this.' I mean, that's how he talked. He was never awed. James Brown, bad-ass James Brown, was who he really was."

When Reagan smiled and asked the entertainer for his suggestions, Brown sat back. "Tell him, Reverend," he said. And so Sharpton, after a stunned pause, ad-libbed a dissertation on the shortcomings of the Reagan administration's domestic policy. After the meeting, Brown gave his protégé some tempered praise. "You need to tighten up your script a little bit," he said, "but you gave him some good ideas."

Sharpton is now, of course, a ubiquitous fixture on American news as a latter-day civil rights crusader. As a "boy-wonder" preacher, he sometimes loitered with friends outside Brown's imposing home in Queens. He became acquainted with Brown while still in his teens and serving as youth director of Operation Breadbasket, the black-empowerment program of the Southern Christian Leadership Conference. Sharpton knew Teddy Brown, the singer's son; when Teddy was killed, Brown took the reverend under his wing. Sharpton had his own emotional hole to fill. When he was a boy, his father had left his mother, forcing her to raise her two children alone. Alfred Charles Sharpton, Sr., had been a big James Brown fan, catching all his shows in New York and emulating his showy pompadours. For the activist, James Brown would become the father figure he never had.

Sharpton, not yet twenty, organized a pair of benefit shows in Teddy's name, renting the former RKO Albee Theatre on DeKalb Avenue in downtown Brooklyn. "It was the biggest night of my life," Sharpton remembers. "Miles Davis came to the show and stood in the wings all night." Onstage, Sharpton presented his new mentor with an award: not gold, not platinum—a symbolic black record.

For a decade, the preacher traveled off and on with the entertainer, joining the singer's small inner circle on his private Lear jet. In 1980 the reverend married Kathy Jordan, one of Brown's backup singers. By the middle of the decade Sharpton had gained plenty of notoriety of his own, orchestrating media coverage to draw attention to the country's lingering racial conflicts and resentments. While he gradually drifted from the singer's everyday orbit, the two men remained close. When Brown received the Lifetime Achievement Award at the Grammys in 1992, the men and their companions left the ceremony prematurely to celebrate amongst themselves at the Stage Deli. At the Kennedy Center Honors in 2003, Brown insisted that the Bush administration provide prominent box seats for Sharpton, who was running as a Democrat for president.

To Brown, the young Al Sharpton was the political voice of the James Brown show. Just as featured singers such as Tammi Terrell, Marva Whitney, and Lyn Collins were Brown's answer to soul superstars like Diana Ross and Aretha Franklin, Sharpton was the singer's "black leader project." Like his long line of stellar sidemen, Brown saw Sharpton as another instrumental voice he could cut in the James Brown mold, then set free to improvise. "In his mind," says the reverend, "I was Maceo or Fred—I was a James Brown Production."

Since his presidential campaign, Sharpton has emerged as something of a kingmaker in American politics. When *New York* magazine described how Barack Obama was vying with Hillary Clinton, the wife of the so-called "first black president," for Sharpton's support in the 2008 Democratic primaries, the reverend invoked his mentor, as he so often does. If Obama's universal, multiracial appeal was making Sharpton's brand of identity politics obsolete, the writer noted, the minister was completely unconcerned. "Ten years ago, they said Colin Powell was going to make Jesse [Jackson] obsolete," Sharpton said. "They've always had a Barack Obama. There will always be a more inside, acceptable black they will say makes us obsolete. I worry about that as much as James Brown worried about Sammy Davis making him obsolete."

*　　*　　*

If Brown's new music was approaching obsolescence, his legend among his fellow entertainers was quickly consolidating. By the 1980s the music industry was utterly dominated by his fans. Among countless others, Michael Jackson, Prince, Bruce Springsteen, Bob Marley, and Miles Davis all acknowledged Brown's tremendous influence. And despite his misgivings about rap, a new generation barely old enough to have firsthand experience with "Think" or "Cold Sweat" saw this middle-aged man in the outrageous stretch jumpsuits as a Homeric character, a mythical hero embodying a whole new idiomatic language.

Afrika Bambaataa, one of the Bronx-based party DJs of the 1970s who helped envision the sampling culture of modern music with their stark juxtaposition of musical styles, was among the first of the hip-hop elders to look to Brown as a patriarch. After serving as a division leader in a South Bronx gang called the Black Spades as a young teenager, the imposing son of West Indian immigrants had an epiphany following a trip to Africa, when he took a Zulu name said to mean "affectionate leader." Bambaataa's new thrust, a group called the Universal Zulu Nation, gave music a central role in reforming the gang culture of the Bronx, and the peace-enforcing DJ was especially inspired by Brown's brand of street-level activism.

The release of "Say It Loud—I'm Black and I'm Proud," Bambaataa once said, was "when we transcend[ed] from Negro to black. Negro to us was somebody who needed to grow into a knowledge of themself [sic]." In 1984 Bambaataa effectively introduced Brown to hip-hop when the Godfather of Soul and the Godfather of Hip-Hop collaborated on a track called "Unity." The two men shared an affinity for mythos and a belief in the restorative power of music—in Bambaataa's case, "stopping bullets with two turntables," as a *Village Voice* writer put it in 1984. "Basically, James gonna live forever," Bambaataa said. "Even when he goes, he gonna keep on ministering."

As much as his innovative music, Brown's front-and-center African-American identity was a distinct inspiration to the upstarts of hip-hop. At a time when ghetto culture was emerging for the first time into the mainstream as a wellspring of style, the singer became an international superstar. He'd made his first trip to Africa in early April 1968, just before King's assassination, at the invitation of the Ivory Coast Ministry of Radio and Television, where he claimed he was paid a record sum for a one-night engagement. In Nigeria in the early 1970s, James Brown albums were ubiquitous talismans. So many young men there carried his records under their arms as a fashion statement that the singer's record company could claim that his album sales in the country were bigger than the actual number of turntables. On a visit to Senegal, schoolboys who spoke no English chanted the singer's name as he arrived on Goree Island by boat in a black beret and dark turtleneck. In Ghana, a popular sweatshirt printed by a political party, the National Alliance of Liberals, paraphrased Mr. Dynamite: "Say It Loud—I'm NAL and I'm Proud!" (Typically stubborn, Brown claimed no particular affinity for the music of Afrobeat pop stars such as Fela Kuti and Orlando Julius, who were undoubtedly influenced by—and, in turn, may well have influenced—Brown's own band.)

In the early 1970s, when the first wave of hip-hop artists were still in their school years, Brown's vast network of local disk jockeys had driven around America's inner cities, passing out copies of his new records to young fans. In Philadelphia, for instance, Sonny Hobson—"The Burner," madly dashing through song introductions and public service announcements on WHAT-AM—cruised the streets in the Sonny Hobson Mobile, passing out complimentary James Brown 45s as if they were the modern-day version of Thomas Paine's *Common Sense.* "I remember my first James Brown record was *Say It Loud*," says Jesse B. Weaver, better known as Schoolly D, one of the many first-generation rappers of the 1980s who owed both their rhythmic emphasis and their social conscience to the Godfather of Soul. Often credited as the original gangsta rapper, Schoolly D called his first self-produced record *Say It Loud, I Love Rap and I'm Proud.* When he began expressing the principled side of his persona, his frame of mind was again unmistakably influenced by Brown: "Get Off Your Ass and Get Involved," as he titled one of the raps on his album *Am I Black Enough for You?* "It would be amazing if somebody is in hip-hop right now, at my age, who didn't grow up listening to James Brown," says Weaver. "What else would they have listened to?"

Both the method and the message spoke loud and clear to the future architects of hip-hop. Besides sampling Brown extensively, Weaver's contemporaries Run-DMC, the first superstar rap group, recorded songs such as "Proud to Be Black" and stressed the importance of education. "We knew we could make education cool," said Darryl "D.M.C." McDaniels. "We knew we could make a difference."

As Brown famously maintained, his crucial innovation was to hear each instrument in his orchestra as another form of percussion. His masterful use of compositional space and the resulting isolation of each element—pistonlike guitar strokes, explosive clusters of electric bass notes, the free-jazz bleating of unleashed horn players, Brown's own laryngeal eruptions—proved ideally suited to the emergent art of sampling. Marley Marl, one of the early innovators in hip-hop production, made James Brown samples an integral part of raps by Big Daddy Kane, Kool G Rap, Eric B. and Rakim, and other formative acts. The confrontational group Public Enemy dipped repeatedly into the well, using a skirling horn from the J.B.s' "The Grunt" to create an atmospheric Armageddon on "Rebel Without a Pause" and the slippery interplay of bass and guitar from the J.B.s' "Hot Pants Road" on the long-hot-summer anthem "Fight the Power." There are three Bs of music, many rappers have claimed: Beethoven, Bach, and Brown. Kurtis Blow has called "Give It Up or Turnit a Loose" "hip-hop's National Anthem." Just as James Brown is believed to be the most sampled artist of all time, Clyde Stubblefield's skittering bass-and-snare beat on the singer's "Funky Drummer" is reputed to be the most sampled loop of all time.

Despite Brown's occasional objections, all of this sampling activity brought the singer untold millions in licensing fees over the years. His popularity, in fact, was so great among rappers and their producers that a James Brown sample was considered too obvious by the early 1990s. "When we got in the game," said Craig Irving, aka Doodlebug, of the good-vibe hip-hop group Digable Planets, which debuted in 1993, "James Brown had gotten looped to the point where it was like, 'Is James Brown real, or does he only exist as something to sample and make a record out of?' "

Brown had already submitted his answer. "I'm real," he growled on one of his last records to claw its way up the R&B chart, a glossy, drum-programmed stab at contemporaneity. "The real Super Bad."

CODA

James Brown's death on Christmas Day, 2006, was followed a day later by the expiration of an ex-president, Gerald Ford. Surely Brown would have been gratified to know that he received a comparable, if not superior, deluge of recognition.

On a chilly, gray day outside Harlem's Apollo Theater, the symbolic birthplace of Brown's own inimitable brand of statesmanship, satellite trucks lined the neighborhood's main artery and scores of photographers jostled to record the arrival of the singer's gold-plated casket, enclosed in a curtained carriage drawn by two massive white horses. Thousands of fans crowded the curb in both directions under the theater's marquee, confined like cattle by police barricades. The two lines wrapped around the corners to the east and west of the theater, weaving well uptown on the parallel north-south boulevards named for

Malcolm X and Adam Clayton Powell. "It wouldn't be a James Brown show if the lines weren't down the block," a middle-aged black man in a biker's leather jacket, his head wrapped in a bandanna, hollered above the din of the helicopters hovering overhead.

Inside, children in church clothes stood obediently with their parents as the line inched toward the body, lying onstage in the open casket amid a profusion of floral arrangements. In death, James Brown seemed impossibly tiny, frail, almost birdlike. Mortality never did suit him. Now, however, despite the realities of the flesh, his presence loomed as large as ever, as the sound system crackled eerily with various live performances recorded in this very room. At the back of the house, those who had paid their respects were being ushered out a side door into the alley. Some lingered, listening to one more song.

"This is an opportunity to educate my son," said a stylish woman with a proper British accent. The boy wore his hair in tiny dreadlocks and a James Brown T-shirt pulled over the collared shirt he'd been asked to wear that morning. Mother and son had seen the singer perform in 2003 at the Royal Albert Hall in London, and the boy had idolized him ever since. He cried profusely when he heard the news of Brown's death. "He felt almost personally related," said his mother.

In front of the theater, a gleaming black SUV made a slow crawl through the commotion beneath the Christmas lights strung across 125th Street, blaring a familiar gloomy ballad. This, cried the raspy voice, was a man's world.

At the time of Brown's death, Kevin White was approaching the advanced stages of Alzheimer's disease. Tom Atkins, having suffered for more than a decade from the onset of amyotrophic lateral sclerosis, or Lou Gehrig's disease, had just a little over a year to live. Syd Nathan, Ben Bart, and Ralph Bass were all dead; so were Ray Charles, Sam Cooke, and Little Willie John. Several of the musicians who had helped shape the sound of Brown's band preceded him to the grave, among them St. Clair Pinckney, Jimmy Nolen, Bernard Odum, and Waymon Reed. Bobby Byrd died nine months after the man he'd spent a lifetime right behind.

As the singer's wives, children, and advisers filed suit and countersuit over his shaky estate, Brown's compound legal troubles all but ensured that he would go on making news for years to come. "The irony is that people are squabbling over things that James Brown created and earned," Al Sharpton said. "He didn't inherit anything. He grew up fatherless, motherless, penniless and left people arguing over what they inherit from him." In his personal life, Brown left a real mess.

In public, however, Papa never did take no mess.

NOTES

OVERTURE

1. "He came on like the aurora borealis": "The Biggest Cat," *Time*, April 1, 1966.
2. Ellington's *Boola: Beyond Category: The Life and Genius of Duke Ellington*, John Edward Hasse (Da Capo, 1995), pp. 260–262.
3. "I still don't like the blues": James Brown with Bruce Tucker, *James Brown: The Godfather of Soul* (Macmillan Publishing Company, 1986), p. 6.
4. "military attitude of the soul": Ralph Waldo Emerson, *Emerson's Essays* (Thomas Y. Crowell Company, 1926), p. 177.
5. "James Brown is a concept, a vibration . . .": Cliff White and Harry Weinger, liner notes, *Star Time* boxed set (Polydor Records, 1991).

1 ■ LOST SOMEONE

1. "He is inside the mind of every player": Elias Canetti, *Crowds and Power* (The Viking Press, 1962), p. 396.
2. "To call somebody black was an insult": quoted in Alan Pomerance, *Repeal of the Blues: How Black Entertainers Influenced Civil Rights* (Citadel Press, 1988), p. ix.

3. "My community was afraid of that word": Dave Zirin, *What's My Name, Fool?: Sports and Resistance in the United States* (Haymarket Books, 2005), p. 93.

4. "When I was growin' up . . .": Cynthia Rose, *Living in America: The Soul Saga of James Brown* (Serpent's Tail, 1990), p. 68.

5. "Dr. King himself wasn't a street person": Brown/Tucker, p. 172.

2 ■ BEWILDERED

1. "I feel very strongly that I was *sent* to Boston": Coretta Scott King, *My Life With Martin Luther King, Jr.* (Henry Holt and Company, 1969; revised 1993), p. 48.

2. a city "that slaves heard about": Emily Hiestand and Ande Zellman, editors, *The Good City: Writers Explore 21st Century Boston* (Beacon Press, 2004), p. 156.

3. "We must get rid of slavery": quoted in Stephen Kendrick and Paul Kendrick, *Sarah's Long Walk: The Free Blacks of Boston and How Their Struggle for Equality Changed America* (Beacon Press, 2004), p. 250.

4. "called themselves the Four Hundred": Malcolm X with Alex Haley, *The Autobiography of Malcolm X* (Grove Press, Inc., 1964), p. 40.

5. "I could go where I pleased": Senator Edward W. Brooke, *Bridging the Divide: My Life* (Rutgers University Press, 2007), p. 23.

6. Boston population figures: George V. Higgins, *Style Versus Substance: Boston, Kevin White, and the Politics of Illusion* (Macmillan Publishing Company, 1984), p. 49.

7. "people programs": ibid., p. 67.

8. *Gone with the Wind*: J. Anthony Lukas, *Common Ground: A Turbulent Decade in the Lives of Three American Families* (Random House, Inc., 1985), p. 29.

3 ■ THINK

The recollections of Tom Atkins and Kevin White are drawn from archival interview footage at WGBH and in the collection of the late filmmaker Henry Hampton.

1. "It was not safe to be a white man in Roxbury": *Boston Herald Traveler*, April 7, 1968.
2. "almost a personal enactment": Marshall Frady, Martin Luther King, Jr. (Lipper/Viking, 2002), p. 206.
3. "the language of the unheard": quoted in Cecil Brown, *Stagolee Shot Billy* (Harvard University Press, 2003), p. 203.
4. Sunday morning strategy sessions: Mel King, *Chain of Change: Struggles for Black Community Development* (South End Press, 1981), p. 103.
5. Kansas City disturbance: *Soul*, December 26, 1966.
6. Solomon Burke incident: Craig Werner, *A Change Is Gonna Come: Music, Race & The Soul of America* (Plume, 1998), p. 83.
7. Joe Tex incident: Scott Freeman, *Otis!: The Otis Redding Story* (St. Martin's Press, 2001), pp. 70–71.
8. "Black radio came of age": Nelson George, *The Death of Rhythm and Blues* (Pantheon Books, 1988), p. 111.
9. Boston Celtics: John Taylor, *The Rivalry: Bill Russell, Wilt Chamberlain, and the Golden Age of Basketball* (Random House, 2005), pp. 303–304.
10. "Now I'm going to play to an empty house": Brown/Tucker, pp. 185–186.
11. "I would have gone on and done the show anyway": ibid., p. 186.

4 ■ BRING IT UP

1. "I'm a model man": *Melody Maker*, February 24, 1973.
2. Bloodlines: Brown/Tucker, p. 2; James Brown with Marc Eliot, *I Feel Good: A Memoir of a Life of Soul* (New American Library, 2005), p. 54.
3. "inconceivable for James Brown to be born and raised . . .": Brown/ Eliot, p. 85.
4. "worked a change in me": Brown/Tucker, p. 5.
5. Dickens on Master Juba: quoted in Samuel A. Floyd, Jr., *The Power of Black Music: Interpreting Its History from Africa to the United States* (Oxford University Press, 1995), p. 55.

6. "I was much better at baseball than singing": Brown/Tucker, p. 26.
7. "I'd be out there stumbling around": ibid., p. 27.
8. "When I get out of here . . .": ibid., p. 34.
9. "The fighters were about twenty-three": quoted in Suzanne E. Smith, *Dancing in the Street: Motown and the Cultural Politics of Detroit* (Harvard University Press, 1999), p. 70.
10. "I'd *sing* 'em sometimes": Brown/Tucker, p. 17.
11. "Louis Jordan was the first recording artist . . .": quoted in Bill Milkowski, *Swing It!: An Annotated History of Jive* (Billboard Books, 2001), pp. 47–54.
12. *Silas Green from New Orleans*: Errol Hill and James Hatch, *A History of African-American Theater* (Cambridge University Press, 2003); www.circusinamerica.org.
13. Bishop Daddy Grace: Marie W. Dallam, *Daddy Grace: A Celebrity Preacher and His House of Prayer* (New York University Press, 2007), pp. 1, 2, 49, 56.
14. "He was like a god on earth": Brown/Tucker, p. 19.

5 ■ TRY ME

1. "I knew I couldn't be too aggressive": Brown/Eliot, p. 5.
2. "A few hip whites came": Brown/Tucker, p. 144.
3. "Blackness seen through black eyes": Langston Hughes, "Writers: Black and White," in Abraham Chapman, editor, *Black Voices: An Anthology of Afro-American Literature* (Mentor, 1968), p. 621.
4. "Some of the worst bigots": Pomerance, p. 154.
5. "No one would want to listen to me": Smith, p. 152.
6. Booker T. Washington: Mike Marqusee, *Redemption Song: Muhammad Ali and the Spirit of the Sixties* (Verso, 1999), p. 19.
7. "packs of black-leather boys": Nick Tosches, *Hellfire* (Delacorte Press, 1982), p. 146.
8. "I am not against rock 'n' roll as such": Glenn C. Altschuler, *All Shook Up: How Rock 'n' Roll Changed America* (Oxford University Press, 2003), pp. 3–4.
9. "The blacks on one side, whites on the other": Brian Ward, *Just My*

Soul Responding: Rhythm and Blues, Black Consciousness, and Race Relations (University of California Press, 1998), p. 130.

10. "By their newfound attachment to rhythm and blues": quoted in Altschuler, p. 17.

11. "How better to understand": quoted in Altschuler, p. 48.

12. "In many ways . . .": Brown/Eliot, p. 48.

13. "saga of the black man in America": Dave Marsh, *The Heart of Rock & Soul: The 1001 Greatest Singles Ever Made* (Plume, 1989), p. 294.

14. "should not be treated like he's the world's first public figure . . .": Peter Guralnick, *Sweet Soul Music: Rhythm and Blues and the Southern Dream of Freedom* (Little, Brown and Company, 1986), p. 556.

16. "Our hearts really throbbed": Guralnick, pp. 523–524.

17. "integrated themselves": Brown/Tucker, p. 146.

18. "You must not know where Bop comes from": Chapman, p. 104.

19. Abbey Lincoln: Peniel E. Joseph, *Waiting 'Til the Midnight Hour: A Narrative History of Black Power in America* (Henry Holt and Company, 2006), pp. 39–40.

20. "Especially in black America": Ward, p. 324.

21. "a man trying to fight his way out of a fog": Marsh, p. 97.

22. "programs that are so out of sight": quoted in Shaw, pp. 259–260.

23. "When people talk about soul music": Brown/Tucker, p. 120.

24. "I was hearing everything": Brown/Tucker, p. 158.

6 ■ COLD SWEAT

1. "Keep Cool": Ted Vincent, *Keep Cool: The Black Activists Who Built the Jazz Age* (Pluto Press, 1995), p. 131.

2. "stay off the streets": Joseph, pp. 227–228.

3. Vote White: Brooke, p. 69.

4. "Why would I go back . . . ?": ibid., p. 6.

5. "once ran successfully for reelection": ibid., p. 55.

6. "You're not black": ibid., p. 174.

7. "too much power for one man": Joseph, pp. 9–10.

8. "shout" music: Dallam, p. 63.
9. "shouts, and groans, terrific shrieks": quoted in Barbara Ehrenreich, *Dancing in the Streets: A History of Collective Joy* (Metropolitan Books/Henry Holt and Company, 2006), p. 3.
10. "I know hardship": *Jet*, December 26, 1966.

7 ■ SOUL PRIDE, PT. 1

1. "I worked to get these people the right": quoted in Drew D. Hansen, *The Dream: Martin Luther King, Jr. and the Speech That Inspired a Nation* (Ecco/HarperCollins, 2003), p. 185.
2. "I'm a racist when it comes to freedom": quoted in Arnold Shaw, *The World of Soul: Black America's Contribution to the Pop Music Scene* (Cowles Book Company, Inc., 1970), pp. 259–260.
3. "It's a little beyond me right now": *Star Time* boxed set.
4. "sometimes bleak, often tormented": David Rosenthal, *Hard Bop: Jazz & Black Music, 1955–1965* (Oxford University Press, 1992), p. 63.
5. "Fire! That's what people want": ibid., p. 73.
6. "This album belongs in the home": Smith, p. 23.
7. "I'm a dropout": *Jet*, December 26, 1966.
8. "That was one of the things I most wanted": Brown/Eliot, p. 82.
9. Stax Records and "Stay in School" campaign: Michael Haralambos, *Soul Music: The Birth of a Sound in Black America* (Da Capo, 1985); reprint of *Right On! From Blues to Soul in Black America* (Eddison Press, 1974), p. 131.
10. "This is the twenty-seventh time": Joseph, p. 147.
11. "coalition of conscience": David Garrow, *Bearing the Cross: Martin Luther King, Jr., and the Southern Christian Leadership Conference* (William Morrow & Company, 1986), p. 484.
12. "Who the hell ever said I was nonviolent?": *New York Times*, June 8, 1966.
13. "Racism is racism": Joseph, p. 149.
14. "To some people it meant black pride": Brown/Tucker, p. 169.
15. "You are *somebody*": Frady, p. 108.
16. "I wanted to throw the radio down": Smith, 169.

17. "You'd hear Aretha": quoted in Werner, p. 121.

18. "I got the sense that James": Fred Wesley, *Hit Me, Fred: Recollections of a Sideman* (Duke University Press, 2002), p. 93.

19. "the 'hunh' that punctuates the poem": John Russell Rickford and Russell John Rickford, *Spoken Soul: The Story of Black English* (John Wiley & Sons, Inc., 2000), p. 18.

20. "James Brown said, 'I'm gonna express myself' ": *James Brown: Soul Survivor* (documentary).

21. "lu-fuki": Robert Palmer, *Rock 'n' Roll: An Unruly History* (Harmony Books, 1995), p. 239.

22. " 'Cold Sweat' deeply affected the musicians": quoted in Rickey Vincent, *Funk: The Music, the People, and the Rhythm of the One* (St. Martin's Griffin, 1996), p. 123.

23. "You could use your ears": *San Francisco Classical Voice*, www.sfcv. org.

24. "People wondered for years": www.redbullmusicacademy.com.

25. "That . . . was real black power": Brown/Tucker, pp. 178–179.

8 ■ THINGS GOT TO GET BETTER

1. "It was kind of pretty": *Mojo*, July 2003.

2. "I did it all": Jim Payne, *Give the Drummers Some! The Great Drummers of R&B, Funk & Soul* (Face the Music Productions, 1996).

3. "I think she was the strongest": Brown/Tucker, p. 192.

4. "A colored man is a man . . .": *Billboard*, September 20, 1969.

5. "A can of Red Devil lye": Malcolm X, pp. 52–55.

6. "We have to stop being ashamed": quoted in William L. Van Deburg, *New Day in Babylon: The Black Power Movement and American Culture, 1965–1975* (University of Chicago Press, 1992), p. 201.

7. "The man spent more time in curlers": *Rolling Stone*, January 25, 2007.

8. "an indescribably fast and furious combination": *Dance*, August 1, 2000.

9. "People who truly dance": Pearl Primus, "African Dance," in Kariamu Welsh Asante, editor, *African Dance: An Artistic, Historical and Philosophical Inquiry* (Africa World Press, Inc., 1996), pp. 3–10.

9 ■ GET IT TOGETHER

1. "It made me feel terrible": Brown/Tucker, p. 15.
2. Gorgeous George: Brown/Tucker, p. 106.
3. "a rehearsal onstage of the succor . . .": *Rolling Stone*, June 29, 2006.
4. "James Brown, the noted rock 'n' roll performer": *Wall Street Journal*, April 10, 1968.
5. "People still ask me": Brown/Eliot, 149–150.
6. "how he made a crucial moment": *Newsweek*, December 28, 2006.
7. "Sixty percent of the looters": *Life*, April 19, 1968.
8. forty-five million dollars: Joseph, p. 227.
9. giving away free beer: Kenneth O'Reilly, *Nixon's Piano: Presidents and Racial Politics from Washington to Clinton* (The Free Press, 1995), O'Reilly, p. 339.
10. "You won't get one like this": Ben W. Gilbert and the Staff of the *Washington Post, Ten Blocks from the White House: Anatomy of the Washington Riots of 1968* (Frederick A. Praeger Publishers, 1968), p. 23.
11. "it seemed as if we were experiencing": O'Reilly, p. 272.
12. "By that time I had received several requests": Brown/Tucker, pp. 188–189.
13. "I know how everybody feels": Gilbert, p. 108.
14. "I think that was an audience": Brown/Tucker, p. 189.
15. "greatest country in the world": Shaw, p. 256.
16. "a major contribution": *Billboard*.
17. Boston damage: *Boston Globe*, April 7, 1968.
18. "Your immediate willingness to televise": Hartford Gunn speech, WGBH archive.
19. "I don't know what happened to The Man": *Bay State Banner*, April 11, 1968.

20. "I think there's been one thousand percent improvement": ibid.
21. "We started talking to the young people": *Boston Herald Traveler.*
22. "People didn't go home": Mel King, pp. 104–106.
23. "Well, gentlemen, the city is at stake here": Lukas, pp. 35–43.
24. "one of the darkest hours": Stephen B. Oates, *Let the Trumpet Sound: A Life of Martin Luther King, Jr.* (Harper & Row Publishers, Inc., 1982), pp. 494–498.

10 ■ IT'S A NEW DAY

1. "Every day is history to me": *Newsweek*, July 1, 1968.
2. King funeral: David Levering Lewis, *King: A Biography* (University of Illinois Press, 1970), p. 390; Oates, p. 495.
3. Funeral of Otis Redding: Guralnick, pp. 327–328.
4. "The hard, driving shouting": Amiri Baraka, "The Changing Same (R&B and New Black Music)," in William J. Harris, editor, *The LeRoi Jones/Amiri Baraka Reader* (Thunder's Mouth Press, 1991), pp. 190–191.
5. "Certainly his sound is 'further out' ": ibid., p. 208.
6. "Say It Loud": Brown/Tucker, p. 124.
7. "James Brown knows the problems we have": Haralambos, p. 108.
8. "It was a black man by the name of Simon": Rev. Jasper Williams, *I'm Black and I'm Proud* (Jewel-Paula Records, 1994; sound recording).
9. "For those of you who are black": quoted in Schulman, p. 3.
10. "I was the one who made the dark-complexioned people popular": Brown/Tucker, p. 124.
11. "The Black Panthers hated me": Ted Fox, *Showtime at the Apollo: 50 Years of Great Entertainment from Harlem's World-Famous Theatre* (Holt, Rinehart and Winston, 1983), p. 192.
12. "All art must reflect the Black Revolution": quoted in Werner, p. 120.
13. "I do not care a damn for any art that is . . .": W.E.B. Du Bois, "Criteria of Negro Art" (NAACP annual conference address, 1926).
14. "There is no explanation": *Muhammad Speaks*, July 19, 1968.

15. "What many of us over the years": ibid., September 6, 1968.

16. "Clyde Shubble": Brown/Eliot, p. 156.

17. Bob Hope: Brown/Tucker, pp. 191–192.

18. "I knew that the black soldiers were complaining": Mojo.

19. "In my room, the window . . .": ibid.

20. "There were riots over the music": Wallace Terry, Bloods: An Oral History of the Vietnam War by Black Veterans (Random House, 1984), pp. 13–15.

21. "The death of Martin Luther King": Mojo.

22. "That was the best that band ever sounded": ibid.

23. "I was carrying the pride of America": Augusta Chronicle, December 25, 2006.

24. "What really hurt me": Soul, November 18, 1968.

25. "The only thing left for me": Soul, August 26, 1968.

26. "I've been acting as a spokesman": Soul, September 9, 1968.

27. "I've found that if you just keep working": Soul, May 20, 1968.

11 ■ IT'S TOO FUNKY IN HERE

1. "A lot of people still didn't understand it": Brown/Tucker, p. 202.

2. "Being from Georgia": ibid., p. 201.

3. "they have no legal boundaries over me": ibid., p. 206.

4. "overtures to the gentleman on my right": Jet, August 15, 1968.

5. "sense of resynchronizing his body language": Rose, p. 65.

6. "He had invented celebrations": Higgins, p. 2.

7. "Whoever it was appeared": ibid., pp. 149–150.

8. "desperate grab-bag trip": Hunter S. Thompson, Fear and Loathing: On the Campaign Trail '72 (Fawcett Popular Library, 1974), pp. 370–371.

9. "flea market of racism": Bill Russell with Taylor Branch, Second Wind: The Memoirs of an Opinionated Man (Random House, 1979), p. 183.

10. obligation to "orchestrate the city": Higgins, p. 187.

11. "White has survived less because of . . .": ibid., p. 216.

12. "I never met anything like James Brown": WGBH archival footage.

12 ■ REALITY

1. "most important black man in America?": *Look*, February 18, 1969.
2. "the kind that is achieved": Werner, p. 17.
3. Nixon and black enterprise: Bruce J. Schulman, *The Seventies: The Great Shift in American Culture, Society, and Politics* (Da Capo Press, 2001), pp. 23, 25, 37; Dean Kotlowski, "Black Power—Nixon Style," *Business History Review*, September 22, 1998.
4. "I believe in the dignity of man": *Rolling Stone*, August 23, 1969.
5. "That'll just make people madder": Brown/Tucker, p. 210.
6. "Jockey" Jack Gibson: George, p. 446.
7. "I tried to make the same point": Brown/Tucker, p. 211.
8. "I'm from Augusta": *Variety*, May 20, 1970.
9. "I'd like to think that our getting to know each other": Brown/Eliot, p. 143.
10. "He would chastise and counsel his employees": Wesley, p. 96.
11. remained the highest-paid black entertainer: Fox, p. 288.
12. "a lesson to those performers": *Variety*, October 18, 1972.
13. "You always risk losing money": Cal Fussman, *After Jackie: Pride, Prejudice, and Baseball's Forgotten Heroes: An Oral History* (ESPN Books, 2007), p. 198.

13 ■ UNITY, PT. 1

1. "People wear leaders out": Frady, p. 212.
2. "A hundred years from now": quoted in Van Deburg, pp. 208–211.
3. "I had to prove you could be": quoted in Steve Estes, *I Am a Man! Race, Manhood, and the Civil Rights Movement* (University of North Carolina Press, 2005), p. 100.
4. "It can be pretty scary": Doon Arbus, "James Brown Is Out of Sight," in Jonathan Eisen, editor, *The Age of Rock: Sounds of the American Cultural Revolution* (Vintage, 1969), p. 290.
5. Cincinnati riot: Philip Gourevitch, "Mr. Brown: On the Road with His Bad Self," in *The New Yorker*, July 29, 2002, pp. 61–64.
6. "Ten years ago, they said": *New York*, December 24, 2007.

7. "When we transcended from Negro": David Toop, *Rap Attack 2: African Rap to Global Hip Hop* (Serpent's Tail, 1991), p. 58.

8. Nigeria record sales: *Billboard*, September 25, 1971.

9. Ghana's National Alliance of Liberals: *Down Beat*, February 18, 1971.

10. "We knew we could make education cool": Brian Coleman, *Check the Technique: Liner Notes for Hip-Hop Junkies* (Villard, 2007), p. 398.

11. "When we got in the game": ibid., p. 165.

CODA

1. "The irony is that people are squabbling": Associated Press, December 25, 2007.

ACKNOWLEDGMENTS

The truth, as they say, can be stranger than fiction. James Brown: no way could you make him up. Telling the story of this definitive moment in the Hardest Working Man's very large life could not have been done properly without the help of many kind souls, and a few key individuals in particular.

Of the vast number of James Brown associates I tracked down, rounded up, badgered, implored, and, in many cases, actually interviewed, Pee Wee Ellis, Marva Whitney, and Fred Wesley—three of the surviving members of the Revue who played the Boston Garden concert in April 1968—were especially gracious with their time and their recollections. Alan Leeds, who has a Ph.D. in JB, read much of the book in draft form and was thoroughly encouraging, instructive, and full of great advice. Chuck D agreed without hesitation to write the Foreword, which booms, as Chuck's work always does, with the voice of authority.

In Boston, Kay Gibbs was a tremendous help, recommending sources and making contacts on my behalf.

The library staff of Washington University in St. Louis provided an illuminating interview that the late filmmaker Henry Hampton conducted with Tom Atkins.

Thanks to my editor, Patrick Mulligan, for his superb recommendations. Thank you to my agent, Paul Bresnick, for fielding my missives and believing that I might actually be able to keep doing this. I couldn't have uncovered half as many indelible images without the tireless efforts of my photo editor, Billie Porter.

Thanks to Peter Guralnick for moral support, and to John and Korki Aldrich for the same on a more personal level. To Lise and David and Rebecca and Scott—you all got it, right away. Brian Coleman lent his eyes and his encouragement. And Bill Crandall is a gentleman and a (pop) scholar.

My wife, Monica, isn't simply my better half—she and the kids, Sam, Will, and Owen, are the whole thing.

Finally, I'd like to thank the Godfather of Soul himself, whose sheer dynamism was a huge inspiration long before this book idea got up in my face. I'd been trying to arrange an interview with him for this project when my father came over at dawn on Christmas morning, bearing the news that Mr. Brown had just died.

Years before, I'd interviewed the singer at an old vaudevillian movie theater in San Francisco. He wanted to catch his own cameo in an eminently forgettable flick. Eating popcorn with the man who invented the Popcorn—*that's* a moment you don't forget.

INDEX